MARKETBUSTERS

MarketBusters

40 STRATEGIC MOVES
THAT DRIVE EXCEPTIONAL
BUSINESS GROWTH

RITA GUNTHER McGRATH
IAN C. MacMILLAN

HARVARD BUSINESS SCHOOL PRESS
BOSTON, MASSACHUSETTS

Library of Congress Cataloging-in-Publication Data

McGrath, Rita Gunther.
   MarketBusters : 40 strategic moves that drive exceptional business growth / Rita Gunther McGrath, Ian C. MacMillan.
      p. cm.
   ISBN 1-59139-123-7 (hardcover: alk. paper)
   1. Strategic planning—Handbooks, manuals, etc. 2. Customer relations— Management—Handbooks, manuals, etc. I. Title: 40 strategic moves that drive exceptional business growth. II. MacMillan, Ian C., 1940– III. Title.
   HD30.28.M3838 2005
      658.4'012—dc22

                                                                    2004023600

There was Helge, who completed a groundbreaking PhD and mowed the lawn when women didn't *do* things like that; who greatly enjoyed the occasions when her only granddaughter matched her daughter's behavioral standard; and who "worried a lot."

There was Wolfgang, who could never resist a good book, who was one of the first people to "get" that a mouse was not a rodent, and whose boundless curiosity encouraged me to "go find out."

There was Moninna, who despite every reason to doubt it, passionately believed that women who took initiative would succeed, and who has created and sustained a place of renewal and comfort for our family.

There was David, who never let obstacles, disappointments, or the cruelty of others infect him with bitterness and who never tired of shaping the world around him, brilliantly.

To the "inlaws and outlaws" who shaped our past, share our present, and will always be part of what we become in the future: Helge, Wolfgang, Moninna, and in memory of David, this book is lovingly dedicated.

—*Rita McGrath*

To three people whom Jean and I wish were here to read this dedication: Joan and Ken MacMillan and Guy Crosby; and to Gladys Crosby, who mercifully will get to read it.

—*Ian MacMillan*

113127

CONTENTS

1

MARKETBUSTING STRATEGIES

T HE FOCUS OF THIS BOOK—strategic growth—is one of the most vital, fascinating, and poorly understood of business processes. We spend most of our research energy trying to make it less mysterious and to help executives manage it more effectively. In our first book, *The Entrepreneurial Mindset,* we emphasized helping managers in large, established companies learn from the practices of habitual entrepreneurs—people who are in the habit of creating new businesses over and over again. We argued in that book that half the battle is using appropriate leadership disciplines—recognizing, for example, that new initiatives need to be managed more like options and less like established businesses.[1] In the time since *The Entrepreneurial Mindset* was published, much has changed. The Internet bubble burst, leading new ventures to fall off the agenda at many companies, in favor of a "back to basics" approach.

Nonetheless, the fundamental issue of where you are going to find new sources of growth hasn't gone away. You know that if you don't innovate and change in the long run you'll be too weak to compete. So, where will your company find new opportunities? How will you as an executive enhance your own potential for career success? How will you sustain the interest of top-quality people? How will you take advantage of changing markets and competitive conditions?

MarketBusters is our effort to provide you with some practical answers. Our hope is that this book will land on your bookshelf (or, even better, in your lap) together with several other excellent books that to us represent the state of the art in understanding growth through new business development. Like Clayton Christensen's *The Innovator's Dilemma* and his and Michael Raynor's *The Innovator's Solution*, this book gives you a point of departure for thinking about growth.[2] Unlike those books, this one focuses on some specific types of opportunities and how you can move to capture them. Think of the books as complementary.

What is a marketbusting move? It's an action taken by your firm that changes the game to deliver markedly superior performance. We've discovered that with the right guidelines, people often surprise themselves by finding that identifying opportunities isn't all that hard. This book is about helping you learn the techniques. We've distilled our observations from a three-year research program into a set of forty moves, clustered around five core strategies that you can use to create marketbusters. One thing that makes this book different is that we have also examined companies that tried, but failed.

Expect to find specific tools, checklists, and techniques, as well as the examples that make them come alive. Expect to find the practical concepts derived not only from our research but also from our attempts over the past three years to apply the tools to real companies facing real dilemmas of growth and differentiation. Where we can, we'll share with you some of our experiences. Where we can't (for reasons of confidentiality), we'll illustrate the techniques with examples from our case study database.

Where MarketBusters Come From

The core of this book involves five strategies to create marketbusters. We developed these strategies after an extensive analysis of forty moves used by firms to successfully transform their market spaces.

We begin with the least difficult idea: to examine the entire set of linked activities customers engage in when they do business with you with the goal of changing the customers' experience. If you figure out how to improve their experience, you can be richly rewarded. Next, we suggest you take a hard-nosed look at how your products and services stack up against the competition. Although this is a tad more challenging —because changes usually involve changing internal processes—at least you have a basis of experience to go on. Slightly more challenging is a strategy of radically changing some factor that drives performance in your industry, either to significantly boost your numbers or to help your customers become more competitive in their markets.

Up to this point, you are basically working from a platform of experience. With the final two strategies, you'll move into new spaces, and thus the final two strategies are the most ambitious. The first involves capitalizing on or sparking a major upheaval in your industry. The second is to identify and exploit what (for you) are radically new opportunity spaces. As you'll see, the strategies increase in difficulty and risk as you work your way through the book.

Two of the strategies—transforming the customers' experience and transforming your offerings—may be familiar because we've explored them in other contexts.[3] In our new research, we found that they are powerful for finding a number of our moves and that we had not really done them justice in earlier works. Three of the strategies—redefining profit drivers, exploiting industry shifts, and creating radically new offerings for your company—are published here for the first time. Table 1-1 summarizes the five approaches.

TABLE 1-1

A Framework for MarketBusters

Lens	Strategy	Tool
Customers	Transform the customers' experience	Consumption chain analysis
Products and offerings	Transform your offerings	Attribute mapping
Key metrics	Redefine profit drivers	Unit of business analysis
Industry shifts	Exploit industry shifts	Industry shifts framework
Emerging opportunities	Enter new markets (to you)	Tectonic triggers framework

Each approach leads you to look for opportunities in a slightly different way. The first approach: Examine your customers' total experience with a view to transforming it. This strategy helps you to identify ways (often surprisingly simple ones) to radically improve the customers' experience of getting their needs met, ideally ways that favor you. We introduced the consumption chain tool in our first book but stopped short of showing you how to make reconfiguration of the consumption chain a centerpiece of your strategy. Here, we use consumption chain analysis as a lens to help you identify how you might be able to capitalize on opportunities by changing your customers' experiences.

The second approach: Transform your products and services by identifying opportunities to add features, eliminate features, or break apart offerings to reach different customer segments. Here we pick up another tool from our first book—*attribute mapping*—but we use it in a dramatically different way. We found that attribute mapping can be used to do more than introduce improvements to existing designs. It can also be used to substantively redesign what you offer.

The third approach: Redefine the metrics that drive profits by radically changing one or more key variables that reflect the standards of competition in your industry. This strategy leads you to discover ways to dramatically change the way you do business or, even better, to dramatically improve the way your customers do business by doing business with you. Here, we introduce a tool we call the *key metrics* analysis to help you discover marketbusting opportunities.

The fourth approach: Exploit more or less predictable shifts in your industry. This strategy calls for you to take advantage of big changes in your industry, either by being the first to spot the change, by taking advantage of second-order effects, or by actively provoking a change yourself. The *industry shifts* framework is a powerful tool for developing strategies using this approach.

The fifth approach: Capture emerging opportunities. This strategy calls for you to identify specific emerging opportunities by looking at the patterns of slow but significant changes in the context in which your business competes. We suggest ways you can anticipate and prepare for the changes and ways to capitalize on the opportunities big changes always create. Unlike the industry lens, this lens often reveals opportunities that are not relevant to the industry as it stands but rather can provide the basis for large step-outs. We introduce here a *tectonic triggers* framework to help you identify emerging opportunities.

About Our Research

We began by defining a *marketbuster*:

1. A 2 percent change (gain or loss) in market position (typically volume share) of an incumbent as a result of its move or the moves of another player.

2. Annual growth in sales of shipments of 10 percent or more over at least two years from a new entry by an innovator.

3. Annual sales or shipment growth 5 percent greater than the growth in the underlying market by an incumbent.

Then we collected examples—as many as we could find, from as many varied contexts as we could find—of firms that tried to make transformational moves to reconfigure the profit streams in their industry. We included examples of failed moves to add to the robustness and replicability of our conclusions and to avoid the antifailure bias that is pervasive in much management writing.[4]

Eventually, we identified certain patterns in the data. Over time, we isolated forty potential moves that companies can make to dramatically reconfigure the profit streams in their industries.

The dilemma was that the patterns alone seemed fairly idiosyncratic to the companies and industries in which they emerged. The next step in our analysis was to take the patterns and draw from them a lens, a strategy, and eventually a tool that could frame a process to help you discover one of these patterns. So, for instance, by examining the customers' total experience via a consumption

---

chain analysis, it might become blindingly obvious that some important parallel offering could have enormous influence over actual purchasing patterns. What we did was link each of the patterns we found to a specific lens, so that by using that lens you too can discover patterns of potential marketbusters on your own.

We then began to test our ideas in real situations. Working with companies all over the world, we ran workshops. We found that using the lenses—in combination with the provocative questions listed in each chapter of this book and a modest amount of facilitation—helped companies take a fresh look at their opportunities. Companies in industries that were being written off as hopelessly mature, hopelessly competitive, or doomed were able to quickly identify new ways to look at their markets, new ways to serve customers, and new ways to create solutions for which they could be well paid. The process worked in industrial materials, industrial gases, heavy equipment production, financial services, hazardous materials disposition, maintenance, and a host of other situations.

We then summarized the best of the discoveries from field testing and experimenting with real companies facing real strategic quandaries and used them to inform the material in this book.

How to Use This Book

Unlike many business books, this book is not intended to be read cover-to-cover on an airplane (although we'd be thrilled to see you dipping into it in that setting!). Rather, we intend it to support a serious and ongoing effort to drive growth and change in your companies. You will find plenty of stories and, more importantly, time-tested questions and frameworks. Everything we propose you try in this book has been tried out by actual companies in real life.

MarketBusters is structured so that you can quickly get to what interests you, use it, and come back to it as your thought process evolves. Each of our five strategies has its own chapter. We offer one company's example to illustrate the lens, to give you the flavor of how it works. Next we spell out the moves, forty in all, underlying each strategy. Then we give you what we call marketbuster *prospecting questions* that you can use to identify ideas that your company can use. The questions are clearly set off from the text so that you can quickly find them when you come back to the book. At the end of each chapter, we provide a summary of action steps you can take to use the strategy effectively. At the end of the book, you'll find a catalog of all the moves and the provocative questions associated with them, to make it easy for you to find them.

Where should you start? It depends on the business challenges you face. Have the feeling that things are too stable and static in your markets and that they may be ripe for change? Start with chapter 2. Struggling to differentiate yourself from competitive offerings? Chapter 3 offers ideas for renewal, based on a tough-minded perspective on how you compete. Believe that new technologies or approaches might radically change your value chain? Chapter 4 offers some guidance for making potential opportunities pay off. In an industry in the middle of a transformation or under significant cyclical pressures? Try chapter 5. And if you believe that the time has come for your company to make a major move into a new opportunity space, you'll find ideas in chapter 6.

We don't mean to imply that making a marketbusting move is easy. If it were, smart competitors would already be out there doing it. The big challenge is not only coming up with the ideas but also making them happen. So in chapter 7, we deal with implementation issues. We describe how you'll need to align the key organizational elements to execute a marketbusting strategy effectively, and we alert you to possible barriers and minefields you need to be wary of as you move to implementation. In this chapter, too, we suggest a simple analytical tool, the *delay and resistance analysis table* (which we affectionately call DRAT). This table is a simple way of making sure that you have thought comprehensively about execution challenges and are prepared to take them on. Finally, chapter 8 takes you step by step through a case study, so you can see how it all fits together.

Preparing Yourself: Audit Your Strategy and Clarify Your Process

Let's be realistic. Your organization probably has some kind of strategy and is trying every day to outpace the competition and satisfy its customers. We recognize that marketbusters must fit into some process that your company already uses to create strategy. Nonetheless, judging from our experience in executive courses and workshops, we continue to be surprised at how many organizations seem to lack a coherent process for developing and executing strategy.

So at the risk of asking you to repeat Strategy 101 but in the interest of being pragmatic and realistic, we suggest that you audit your company's strategy before you start trying to implement a marketbusting move. This approach will give you a baseline. If you already have good processes in place, you should be able to zip through the audit in no time. If not, you may want to revisit your base strategy. After you've taken a good hard look at what you're doing now, you'll be ready to start building marketbusting moves into the way you "do strategy."

Your Strategy Audit

The following checklist is a simple way to assess the clarity, robustness, and health of your strategy as it stands. It's a good idea to get in touch with your existing strategy before contemplating the kinds of major shifts that marketbusting implies.

Objectives

- What outcome represents success for this strategy? How clear and well articulated is it?

- Is it clear which market arenas are desirable and undesirable? Is the strategic logic for this choice clear and unambiguous? Do you use a screening mechanism to include desirable arenas or activities and exclude undesirable ones?

- Has the strategy been translated to memorable, simple phrases and idioms that have emotional resonance for employees?

- Do you have a systematic approach to communication that ensures widespread understanding of the strategy?

- Does your company have a way of describing the strategy to key financial stakeholders (such as stock analysts)?

Customers or Clients

- Which customers does your business seek to serve, and in what priority order? Why have you chosen these customers? Which customers do you not seek to serve? Why?

- What does your business do that offers a winning proposition for customers, consisting of greater value than is offered by competitors, in such a way that customers will pay for this greater value? How does your offering add value, from the point of view of the customer? Describe this value in a few sentences.[5]

- How is the business capturing value for your company from the target customers?

Competitors

- Who are they? Are you obtaining competitive intelligence about all three categories of competition? By this we mean not only the traditional competitors that you know well, but also potential competitors who might be preparing to attack you as well as oblique competitors—those who are in competition with you for something that you need, such as investment capital or disposable time. Is there a clear competitive strategy in place for each category?

- What is the form of competitive insulation—that is, how do you protect your chosen markets from the competition?

- What moves are competitors most likely to make? How will you respond?[6]

- How do you currently conduct competitive intelligence? How will your leaders get decent information about what the competitors are doing?

Complementors (business partners, or those whose cooperation you need to make your business work)

- Which activities do you perform on your own (without a partner)? Does partnering create future liabilities (such as losing touch with customers or weakening the technological or capability base of your business)?

- Whom do you need in your network of stakeholders to stay effective? Has a solid stakeholder analysis been done? When was it last updated?

- Do you have a continuously updated list of potential targets for acquisitions or potential partners for alliances? Do you have a clear strategy for post-alliance or acquisition management?

Company and Capabilities

- What are the unique capabilities and competencies of your business? How are they being leveraged?

- What business model is your company pursuing (what do you get paid for, and how does it fit into the industry's value chain)?

- How does your strategy process ensure that you develop new capabilities and terminate those that are obsolete?

- How will you build and maintain the key human capital your business requires?

Context

- What are the environmental and contextual issues that will affect the success of this strategy?

- How will outside forces (regulation, globalization, war) affect the strategy?

As you think through the answers to these questions, note where you think your company's strategy is healthy and which processes you want to keep in place, as well as places where you think changes are needed. Bear these in mind as you continue to develop a concept for marketbusters in your firm.

If you find that you are really struggling with your strategy process, it might be a wise idea to get away from the day-to-day business. Some good options are to take your team to an executive education course, similar to the ones we run at Columbia and Wharton, hold a facilitated management meeting off-site, or just get a "time out" for yourself to focus on these important questions. In our experience, it's extremely hard to reorient your strategy while you are in the rush of ongoing business. We find most busy executives are surprised at how rewarding such time off can be.

Moving On

Now you know what the book is about, where it came from, and how to use it. The next step is to decide where to start. It makes sense to skim through the book more or less as we've written it, with the easier-to-grasp and lower-risk ideas in the beginning, the more ambitious and somewhat more abstract ideas toward the end.

A few points to remember as you begin this journey. Creating marketbusters requires what we refer to as an "entrepreneurial mindset" on your part. What does this mean? It means that you recognize that competition is increasingly about developing new offerings, new ways of doing business, and new solutions—and not fighting your competitors on price.[7] It also means that you need to be prepared to use the appropriate disciplines for moving into uncertain new areas, and you may not be familiar or comfortable with them.[8] These new disciplines will demand that you, as an executive, develop new skills, such as getting better at making decisions that are roughly right, making sense of ambiguous information, and realizing that failure goes hand in hand with taking intelligent risks.[9]

It is also important to remember that no strategy lasts forever. In fact, by the time this book is published, one or more of the companies we cite as having successfully created a marketbuster may well have gotten into trouble. (This is commonly referred to as the *In Search of Excellence* problem.[10]) We are always surprised that people who agree that strategies need to continually change then expect that the companies we cite as examples will succeed with a particular strategy forever. No strategy will go on being successful indefinitely. Competitors will catch up, markets will change, and even companies that had a great idea can stumble when they take their success for granted. This doesn't mean that the experience of these companies offers no important lessons.

After all, competitors aren't stupid. Strategy 101 suggests that any market you demonstrate to be attractive by your success at marketbusting will attract competition. Strong competitors will provoke a strong competitive response, which often will succeed. Further, the very success of a marketbuster can lead to the rigidity, complacency, and embeddedness in the existing state of affairs that defeats once-successful firms.[11] The point of our examples is that the moves meet our criteria for marketbusters and that they help teach valuable lessons about how to identify such opportunities—and not that the companies behind them are somehow infallible. So just because one or another company has gotten into trouble, has been acquired, has been defeated by a competitor, or has run into some other problem doesn't mean that it didn't come up with a powerful move.

Finally, think of your efforts to drive growth and profitability as a journey and not an event. If finding marketbusters is at the top of your agenda, is in your daily conversation, and is supported by your behavior, your peers and subordinates will get the message that you are genuinely interested and enthusiastic about exploring the chance for these opportunities. If, instead, it's the focus of a splashy off-site with a T-shirt as the main take-away, your efforts will only breed cynicism. Make the time for it. Think about making market-busters one of your top priorities. And be proactive about getting stuff off your to-do list to clear the space you need to be successful.

Action Steps

Step 1: Define the objectives for the growth and profitability of your business in the near term and in the longer term. Will your current strategy get you to these objectives?

Step 2: Audit your current strategy using the questions in the strategy audit section presented earlier. Where is your strategy working well? Where is it not working well? What kinds of changes might you need to make?

Step 3: If your current strategy is either lacking or inadequate to achieve your objectives, identify the kind of change that would make a difference—modest or significant. Do you need to take some time off to get this most important process right? When? Where? Who will you use to help you think it through?

Step 4: Define where you are facing your biggest challenge. Is it in understanding customers? Better crafting of product or service design? Improving key operating metrics? Coping with an industry in transition? Figuring out how to make a really big new move? This might suggest which chapter to start with (2, 3, 4, 5, or 6, depending on the challenge).

Step 5: Get started learning about marketbusters!

2

TRANSFORM YOUR CUSTOMERS' EXPERIENCE

Most of your customers or clients really don't care about what you sell. They spend little time even thinking about it. In fact, few of your customers or clients are likely to regard doing business with you as an exciting event. It certainly isn't a highlight in their busy lives. In short, the business issues that seem all-consuming from where you sit often have very little resonance with your customers.

And yet the absolute core of organizational self-renewal is to develop deep insight into what customers do care about and why. In this chapter, we introduce a practical, proven approach to seeing customers the way they see themselves and intelligently tapping into their experiences in order to change their perspective in your favor.[1]

A customer *consumption chain*, as its name implies, represents the linked sets of activities customers engage in to meet their needs, incidentally doing something that might generate a need for consuming something you sell. Typically, a consumption chain begins with a customer's awareness of some kind of need and continues through evaluating alternative choices, selecting a provider, arranging a contract, sorting out payment, using the offering, disposing of it, repurchasing or recontracting, generating word-of-mouth referrals, and the like. Figure 2-1 depicts a typical consumption chain for a manufactured product.

If your company is typical of many, you will have sliced and diced the consumption chain to reflect the specialization of your firm's functional groups. Thus, sales and marketing folks understand the awareness, evaluation, and buying decision links; financial groups understand the payables, credit screening, and billing links; operations people understand what it takes to make the offering work on customers' sites; and so on.

There is nothing inherently wrong with this specialization; after all, it's efficient. The difficulty is that your customers evaluate their total experience with your company as a whole. If you mess up one significant part of the chain, the whole relationship can be in jeopardy, no matter how well the rest of the operation performs. Moreover, if you are working with a piecemeal concept of your customers and your competition has a more holistic view, you can find yourself

FIGURE 2-1

A Consumption Chain for a Manufactured Product

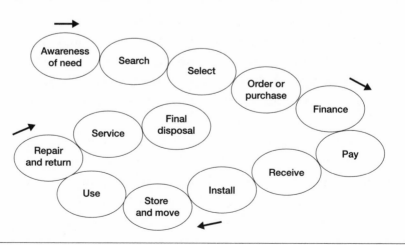

unexpectedly at a major competitive disadvantage if your competitor figures out a way to dramatically improve the overall customer consumption experience.

Let's look at a specific example. Here, a company attempts to revolutionize the way logistics and distribution services are sold and used.

Capitalizing on Insights into Your Customers' Total Experience: Logistics.com

The global shipping and transportation industry accounts for about $3 trillion in expenditures each year.[2] Services were traditionally provided by a fragmented collection of players, including freight forwarding companies, trucking companies, various kinds of brokers competing to fill loads of goods by ship, rail, and other means, and logistics operated in-house by producers. Each supplier focused on its own piece of the total shipping system, leaving customers the task of integrating separate offerings to achieve their goals.

The brainchild of MIT professor Yossi Sheffi, Logistics.com grew from a 1988 concept to achieve marketbuster results. The company created a compelling integrated shipping offering through the use of digital technology. Here's how it works. Traditionally, shippers have sought open bids in an attempt to gain efficiencies (for example, by arranging for use of a single carrier on all three legs of a three-way shipment). A Logistics.com software product, OptiBid, allows shippers to see the impact of various hypothetical routing choices on their costs. In this way, the system encourages carriers to bid more aggressively, based on the prospect of having their costs covered across the complete route. The result is lower total contract prices for shippers and more efficient use of resources by carriers. OptiBid improves the consumption chain for both shippers and carriers rather than only a part of it, as previous approaches did.

Another product, OptiYield, offers decision support for transport providers by giving them real-time information to make cost-saving decisions. Consider a trucking company. To help customers schedule a truck moving across the United States, OptiYield draws on a database of real-time fuel prices, including contract prices for a particular carrier. The trucker might then be advised, for example, to refuel in states having favorable fuel taxes, to change routes based on proximity to cheaper fuel, or to partially fill the tank in anticipation of cheaper fuel availability. Such a decision support system can save trucking firms 6 to 7 percent on fuel costs, which make up about one-fourth of a trucker's total costs. In this low-margin business, the impact on customers' bottom lines is substantial.

When we last obtained independent information for the company, Logistics.com managed more than sixty thousand trucks daily and more than 2.7 million shipments annually. In addition, the company licensed its software to third parties. It achieved a growth rate of 80 percent in the first quarter of 2002, securing twenty-three new deals.

Little of this business represents activity that wasn't being done before in the industry. Instead, Logistics.com has substantially improved its customers' total experience, taking business away from players who focus on only a few links in the chain. In so doing, Logistics.com has discovered ways of capitalizing on cost savings and better service by touching its customers at many links.

Internet Capital Group, the parent company of Logistics.com, sold the assets of the firm to Manhattan Associates on December 31, 2002, for $21.2 million.

The Critical Problem of Mindless Segmentation

Before you can begin to understand the customer's total experience, it's important to consider how you think about sets of customers. We never cease to be amazed by how often companies fail to engage in insightful customer segmentation, relying instead on conventional demographic variables to size their markets and design their offerings. Thus, as table 2-1 shows, companies selling to consumers might develop marketing plans on the basis of customer age, gender, economic status, or geographic location, and business or industrial suppliers might segment their customers on the basis of size, geography, or installation type.

TABLE 2-1

What's Wrong with These Ways of Segmenting Customers?

Customer-Oriented	Business/Industrial-Oriented
Age	Size
Income	Geography
Gender	Installation type
Geography	Channel
Social/ethnic background	Technology
Profession	Location type

There are two problems with using these sorts of segmentation schemes. First, although the segments appear reassuringly quantifiable, demographics seldom accurately reflect customers' idiosyncratic needs or behaviors. Indeed, there is often as much variation in behavior and preference within demographic segments as there is across segments. This means that the purpose for segmenting in the first place—to finely target an offering to customers' specific needs—is not well served.

Second, if you can segment on the basis of demographics, so can everybody else. It's hard to hang onto a competitive advantage if your approach to customers is not differentiated from your competition's. The same market research firms that sell demographic segments to you can sell them to your competition.

We have no particular objection to starting with demographic segments to get a rough idea of how many target customers you might be considering. We encourage you, however, to go beyond this to capture genuine insights about customer behavior. Many companies have enjoyed good results by employing ethnographic, observational, or anthropological approaches to help them best choose how to serve specific customer groups. The goal is to develop insightful segments based on customer behavior rather than on demographic factors. Although you might think this is Marketing 101 (and indeed it is), we continue to observe plenty of companies that don't seem to have taken that course!

Understanding a Customer Segment's Total Experience

Analyzing your consumption chain will also help you to develop differentiated segmentation schemes as you observe that different customer sets behave differently. The goal of a consumption chain analysis is to identify the steps your customers take to satisfy the need they have become aware of (which you can think of as links in the chain), some of which involve their buying something from you.

Some chains are short or simple—for example, the immediate sequence of events that leads a customer to buy chicken nuggets at a fast-food restaurant. Others are long or complex—for example, the sequence of events that leads a steel manufacturer to commission a

FIGURE 2-2

A Consumption Chain for a Service Business

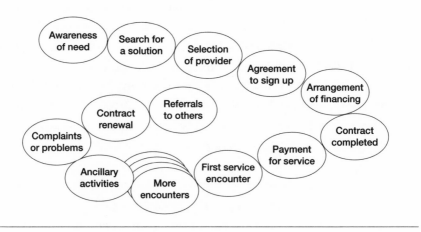

production facility. The point is that the consumption chain of each potential customer offers a starting point that will help you to gain insight into how you might create an offering with marketbusting potential.

Earlier, figure 2-1 showed a typical consumption chain for a manufactured product. A different sequence of activities and links applies to a service offering, as shown in figure 2-2. Note that the "service encounter" link repeats, with each repetition representing an opportunity to either capture or lose favor with the customer.

Developing a Consumption Chain

When you construct a consumption chain, your goal is to capture the most important steps a customer goes through. The goal here is not to be compulsive but rather to get a really good feel for how customers are behaving as they try to get their needs met. It's also important to understand alternative ways customers might behave, because these compete as a way for them to solve their problems.

Before we get into the details of constructing your chain, a few words are in order for those who are in an industry facing fundamental changes. Be aware that industry transformations will show up pragmatically as changes in your customers' experience. For example, consider the plight of companies in the business of producing digital content, such as music or movies. Making money on compact disc (CD) sales used to involve a customer consumption chain like the one in figure 2-3.

What happened to this chain when the potential for purchasing (and swapping) digital music files became a reality? Each link changed. As the links changed, so did the familiar profit model of the CD business. Customers can now easily buy a single song rather than an entire CD to get only the desired song. And, of course, the advent of peer-to-peer music sharing has meant that the "payment" link for some customer segments has disappeared. The chain has been transformed and now looks more like the one depicted in figure 2-4.

FIGURE 2-3

Changing Links in a Transforming Industry: Acquiring Music Analogically

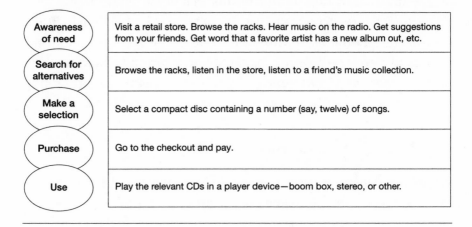

Awareness of need	Visit a retail store. Browse the racks. Hear music on the radio. Get suggestions from your friends. Get word that a favorite artist has a new album out, etc.
Search for alternatives	Browse the racks, listen in the store, listen to a friend's music collection.
Make a selection	Select a compact disc containing a number (say, twelve) of songs.
Purchase	Go to the checkout and pay.
Use	Play the relevant CDs in a player device—boom box, stereo, or other.

FIGURE 2-4

New Links for Acquiring Music Digitally

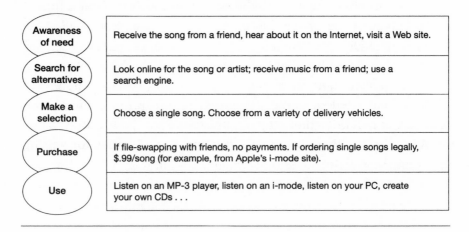

Awareness of need	Receive the song from a friend, hear about it on the Internet, visit a Web site.
Search for alternatives	Look online for the song or artist; receive music from a friend; use a search engine.
Make a selection	Choose a single song. Choose from a variety of delivery vehicles.
Purchase	If file-swapping with friends, no payments. If ordering single songs legally, $.99/song (for example, from Apple's i-mode site).
Use	Listen on an MP-3 player, listen on an i-mode, listen on your PC, create your own CDs . . .

As providers of copyrighted materials ourselves, we aren't wildly enthusiastic about royalty-free content sharing. But when you get beyond the anguish of seeing a profitable business model change drastically, digitization means that some (importantly, not all) customers are clearly interested in a change in the consumption chain for music. Just as this change will make some music models less profitable, it will create tremendous opportunities for others. Several innovative companies—Apple among them—are making a lot of money on alternative ways of distributing music. We can't say what the next dominant model for the music business will be, but we can say with some confidence that the potential for a market-buster is lurking there somewhere.

There are many ways to construct a consumption chain. One we encourage you to try is to assemble a group of people from various functions within your organization. Be sure to include people who are in direct contact with customers: sales, marketing, servicing, credit, complaints, repairs, and technical assistance people. Ask them to draw a chain that reflects the experiences they think your customers have with your company.

When you have a chain identified (or in the case of multiple customer segments, multiple chains), engage representatives from all your major customer segments to help elaborate the chains you have designed. Get them to articulate the links that they experience: Becoming aware, searching, selecting, buying, paying, storing the offering until needed, using, repairing, replacing, upgrading, and disposing are all links that they might experience. Your goal is to determine whether there are marketbusting opportunities for you in changing some aspect of this chain.

For industrial customers, this may be the only way to determine where your offering adds value. Anderson and Narus, for instance, reported on an initiative taken by Alcoa Aerospace in which salespeople were asked to chart all the steps a customer took in acquiring, converting, and disposing of Alcoa offerings. To complete their tasks, the members of the sales force had to gain the cooperation of customer employees and, together, agree on the processes. The exercise proved extremely illuminating for both sides, because cost and benefit elements that had previously been hidden were made explicit. Other observers have found that looking downstream from a pure manufacturing position or extending the core business can yield valuable insights.[3]

How to Construct Your Consumption Chain

- Select a target segment—ideally a segment that you have identified because of its behavior rather than its demographics.

- Identify the people within your company who come into contact with members of that customer segment. (Do you even know who they are?)

- Put together a small task force or discussion group comprising the people in your company who come into contact with this segment.

- Ask them to describe your customers' experience, from the point of initial awareness of need to the point at which a product is exhausted or a relationship ends (or moves to the next stage). Remember that some customers may have different experiences in different contexts. For example, a CEO acquaintance told us about trying to figure out the consumption chain for his high-end grocery stores. He discovered a strong temporal effect. Monday to Friday, his customers were all about efficiency and convenience. Come the weekend, however, and they turned into gourmet shoppers who wanted luxury, choice, and languor in their shopping experience. This prompted the CEO to reset several aisles in his high-end stores each weekend, catering to the specific consumption requirements of these time-pressed would-be gourmets.

- Create a hypothetical consumption chain by taking various "scenes" from a customer's experience as the links, noting what transpires to move a customer from one scene to the next (what we call *trigger events*). Remember: Each business and each segment is likely to have its own way in which the whole chain fits together. Experienced customers, for example, probably become aware they need your offering when something happens to interrupt their experience (such as obsolescence of the existing product or the expiration of a contract or subscription) rather than through advertising.

- Make a critical assessment of how well you are doing at improving that customer's consumption experience. Are there links the customer would prefer to do without? Are there ways you could serve that segment better? Are there things you are offering that the customer doesn't value?

- Consider the provocative questions in the section that follows. What can you do to create a better overall customer experience?

MarketBuster Prospecting

You should now have a good understanding of what your customers are going through. The next step is to use the consumption chain to go prospecting for marketbusters. How can you build on the insights of your analysis to dramatically change something about the way the chain currently works to your advantage? *Marketbuster prospecting* involves asking patterns of provocative questions about how to change the current consumption chain to one that rewrites the rules of the game.

We have identified five marketbusting moves that involve changing the consumption chain.

Move #1: Reconstruct the consumption chain, replacing the existing one with an alternative chain

Move #2: Digitize to combine or replace links in an existing chain

Move #3: Make some links in the consumption chain smarter

Move #4: Eliminate time delays in the links of the chain

Move #5: Monopolize a trigger event

Now let's look at each of these moves in detail.

Move #1: Reconstruct the Consumption Chain

Here you are looking for opportunities to replace an existing consumption chain with a new one that offers a dramatically different experience for the customer. Amazon.com, for example, made headlines by significantly changing almost every link in the book-buying experience, capitalizing on its ability to influence multiple links. For example, it uses customer referrals to enhance the awareness link, adds a new link by offering a "send this book to a friend" feature, makes payment easier via the "one click" payment system, and even makes money by providing a way for you to resell your used volumes.

Example: Found Money from Loose Change. In the early 1990s, the entrepreneurs behind upstart Coinstar, Inc. (founded in 1991), saw an opportunity in the consumption chain having to do with loose change. For many people, the loose change that accumulates on nightstands and kitchen tables is a nuisance. And it's a big problem: Analysts estimate that on average $7.7 billion in pocket change circulates in the United States every year.

Traditionally, to turn that change into more manageable paper bills required a tedious process of sorting the coins, rolling them in paper tubes, and taking them to the bank (during normal banking hours, of course). Some products attempted to address a portion of the problem. Automatic coin sorting machines, for example, allowed users to toss assorted change into a hopper, where a battery-operated device sorted the coins and plopped them into preformed tubes.

Although this solution helped by eliminating the sorting link, it didn't eliminate the hassle of the rest of the links. The coin-sorting machines addressed only a part of the problem.

Coinstar pioneered a new approach that has revolutionized the world of loose change processing: It developed equipment designed to convert loose change to paper cash easily. Coinstar machines, conveniently installed in supermarkets, sort and count the change and issue a coupon that can be used to buy groceries or redeemed for cash at the checkout counter. Think of the impact on the consumption chain: The sorting, rolling, transportation, and refunding links are all eliminated.

Naturally, this service is not free. For a major enhancement in convenience, Coinstar's customers pay a fee of slightly less than 9 percent of the money converted. Isn't that astonishing, when you think about it—that customers would be comfortable paying a substantial fee simply to change the form of the cash they have on hand? And yet, developing a comprehensive solution has created a marketbuster for Coinstar. The company's revenue growth has exceeded 30 percent per year since 2001. In that year alone, Coinstar converted $1.4 billion in coins in more than 9,300 machines. Its revenues for 2003 were $176 million, with projected revenue for 2004 in the range of $178 million to $188 million. Interestingly, Coinstar has also solved a problem for banks, for whom the whole process of dealing piecemeal with consumers' change problems added cost and produced no revenues.

In 2003, Coinstar began offering other payment-related services, such as replenishing prepaid wireless accounts, activating and reloading Truth prepaid MasterCard cards, and enabling employees of participating companies to obtain wage statements, balance inquiries, and other payroll services.

Prospecting Questions for Reconstructing the Consumption Chain

Can links in the existing chain be eliminated or combined with other links?

Can you completely replace this set of links with some other set?

Can you accomplish the same outcome with a different chain?

Can you reshuffle the links to improve your customer's experience?

If parts of the chain are a hassle, can you solve the problem in a different way?

Can you create a complete solution to replace a piecemeal solution?

Move #2: Digitize to Combine or Replace Links in an Existing Chain

An obvious way to change a consumption chain is to use digital technology to alter the way you do business. Although the enthusiasm surrounding this idea during the Internet bubble has been dampened, we believe that many companies have turned away from the real advances in digital technology, most of which are materializing only now that we have a decade of experience with the Internet. And there are plenty of Internet experiments to learn from.

Example: Leverage the Internet to Capture Car Buyers' Attention. CarsDirect.com was founded in 1999 by Scott Painter and Bill Gross (founder of e-commerce incubator idealab!) after Gross's frustrating effort to buy a car online through the referral sites that were the only alternative then available. CarsDirect.com was designed to help the knowledgeable buyer complete the entire purchase transaction—including researching, price negotiation, financing, and delivery—online. Through a network of cooperating dealers, CarsDirect.com can consummate such deals without maintaining inventory or the overhead of physical display spaces. In addition, the company has introduced unprecedented transparency in car pricing with an innovative program that uses statistical models to analyze nationwide price distributions. It sets its price within the lowest 10 percent range of the model being bought.

CarsDirect.com experienced extremely fast growth during its first two years. It reported $15.2 million in sales during 1999 and $491 million during 2000, with annual employee growth of 14.5 percent. In February 2001, CarsDirect.com experienced record levels of traffic, reaching 1.7 million unique visitors and becoming the tenth most visited automotive-related site in July 2001.

CarsDirect.com went on to add new channels to its car-selling business model. Launched in 2001, the CarsDirect Connect referral channel gives shoppers the option of being matched with a member of the CarsDirect.com authorized dealer network. This valuable service connects the customer with a knowledgeable Internet representative at a local dealer, who can provide expert advice and guide the buyer through the car purchase process. In 2002, the company launched its comprehensive UsedCar channel, providing the nation's 30 million used-car buyers with a wealth of free, in-depth research, fast comparison and pricing tools, expert purchase advice, and instant access to more than four hundred thousand late-model cars—all in one convenient online marketplace.

To enhance the original concept of buying new cars online, in September 2002 CarsDirect.com started posting a monthly Best Bargains list. The company's pricing experts select top new vehicle values from among 170,000-plus price configurations available in the marketplace. The CarsDirect.com Best Bargains list is designed to help consumers cut through the clutter of constantly changing manufacturer rebate and incentive offers by presenting a periodic snapshot of exceptional new-vehicle buying opportunities. Rebate and incentive changes are posted to CarsDirect.com's Rebates and Incentives Center as they are published by each automaker. CarsDirect.com is the only multibrand car-buying Web site offering this level of real-world price precision.

Of course, the jury is still out on this attempted marketbuster. For one thing, the competition has begun to emulate the same simplification of the consumption chain by enabling the total purchase rather than a referral. Some early competitors, such as CarOrder. com, have already folded. CarsDirect.com has made further efforts to differentiate the customer experience through development of a research facility and alliances with important complementors such as Bank One for financing. It remains to be seen whether this business model, which calls for a small markup of $50 to $200 on each car sold, will hold in the face of competition and increasing consumer nonchalance about the Internet channel.

What is clear is that CarsDirect.com and its competitors have dramatically changed customer expectations for some important segments by digitizing the experience. The proportion of people buying their cars entirely on the Internet has grown from 2.7 percent in 1999 to 4.7 percent in 2000. International Data Corporation forecast that 7 to 8 percent of sales will be completed online in 2004. An even more interesting change has been the use of online sources for research. Roughly 40 percent of prospective car buyers used the Internet for such purposes in 1999, 54 percent in 2000, and an estimated 60 percent this year.

Example: Making Things Simpler by Eliminating Administrative Hassles. Instead of replacing or eliminating links in the chain, digital technologies can also be used to make the customer experience faster, better, cheaper, or more convenient. In the employee supplemental benefits area, a series of providers, with names such as Eyefinity and BenefitMall.com, have developed services to simplify the administration of employee benefits.

A good example is Colonial Life & Accident Insurance Company, a subsidiary of UnumProvident Corporation. Colonial has focused on the problems employers have in administering supplemental insurance plans. Supplemental plans can be a headache for plan administrators because each employee has unique fund allocations and types of expenditures. Colonial created a special Web site targeted directly at addressing the work of plan administrators with its ColonialConnect for Plan Administrators. More than a thousand employers are now taking advantage of the site's services.

Among the more popular services is EZ Billing, which reconciles corporate benefit bills online at no charge. The plan administrator e-mails Colonial an electronic file showing what payments (based on company records) have been made against the money employees have set aside to cover benefit expenses (usually pretax). Colonial then compares the deduction information to its records and informs the plan administrator of any discrepancies, eliminating a series of reconciliation tasks.

This process greatly reduces the time and hassle of manually reconciling paper invoices or (as had become common among customers) manually entering data to reconcile two incompatible computer systems. A side benefit of this innovation is that the electronic process also reduces errors when compared with manual billing.

Example: Help Customers Deal with Their Logistical Hassles. Other companies have discovered the benefits of using digital technologies to make life easier for their customers. A powerful way to use digital technology, particularly for industrial customers, is to minimize the costs, risks, and time consumed by logistics. This has proved crucial in capital-intensive industries.

Occidental Petroleum has relied on digitization to help it compete with the far larger companies that dominate its businesses: oil and gas exploration and production, and chemicals. Its OxyChem subsidiary, for example, was the first in its industry to embrace the use of electronic technology to create a logistical advantage. It pioneered supply chain connectivity through the Envera network, in which networked trading partners can exchange key transaction data, including purchase orders, order acknowledgment, shipment notification, receipt notification, invoicing, and change orders. The network lowers demand uncertainty, reduces inventory on hand, improves product flow, and minimizes cost.

Prospecting Questions for Digitizing the Chain

Inspect each link in the chain. Can you find ways to deploy Internet, telecommunications, or information technology (IT) and thereby dramatically enhance your offering by

Replacing or combining links?

Improving links by making the customer experience better, cheaper, or more convenient?

Capturing and mining data about the market or about your service delivery?

Better managing your logistics?

Adding new links that customers will be willing to pay for?

Creating new offerings from the information you now collect anyway?

Move #3: Make Some Links in the Consumption Chain Smarter

This technique of hunting for marketbusters involves looking at the links in a consumption chain and asking whether you can add value by making that link smarter. By "smarter," we mean adding intelligent attributes such as recognition, responsiveness, interactivity, or situation-specific calculations to the link. The idea is that value comes from information that you convey to the customer at that link.

You can use any number of electronic technologies to make a link smarter, but smarter does not have to be synonymous with electronics. Gillette's Duracell battery division, for example, figured out how to create a smarter battery by embedding technology that allows a customer to test the battery's charge.

Example: Making Payments Easier Through RFID Technology. Texas Instruments pioneered the use of electronic intelligence when it began commercialization of radio-frequency identification (RFID) technology. TI's RFID tags can be found in such offerings as the ExxonMobil Speedpass, which allows consumers to pay for gas and other sundries without having to swipe a credit card or pay cash. The electronic tags, which can be hooked to a keychain or placed on a credit-card-like plastic card, are linked to a payment system customers have set up in advance, which charges a credit card or other account for the purchase. Mobil (before the merger with Exxon) reported that within the first year of operation, Speedpass-enabled gas stations captured up to 6 percent more market share compared with ordinary gas stations.

Prospecting Questions for Making Links Smarter

Inspect each major link in your consumption chain. Can you find ways of deploying digital intelligence at that link to make your offering

- More responsive?
- Less of a hassle?
- More informative?
- More fine-tuned?
- More user-friendly?
- More convenient?

and thereby dramatically enhance the quality or convenience of the links in your chain?

Can you use digital intelligence to create greater awareness of the benefits you offer at that link?

Can you use digital intelligence to tell you when a customer is at the trigger point for that link?

Move #4: Eliminate Time Delays in the Links of the Chain

Many customers are willing to trade off time for money. This source of marketbusting opportunities requires you to understand how much customer time you're wasting and to develop offerings that eliminate this waste. Alternatively, you might find good ideas by changing the sequencing of events in a consumption chain to create more value.

Example: A Better Beer Experience. Consider an activity as prosaic as buying a beer in a sports stadium. In America, this involves walking to a vendor's location, waiting in a long line, placing your order with one of the waitstaff, finally getting your beer (usually in an extremely annoying and insecure plastic cup with a flimsy lid), and finding your way back to your seat ("excuse me, sorry, excuse me, let me just pass, sorry"), hopefully before you missed anything exciting. Some stadium owners began to try to improve the experience by adding seat-based order takers, but these people added to expenses and didn't really change the majority customer experience because, for the most part, they were stretched too thin to cover all potential customers.

Executives at Amaranth Wireless, a privately held company founded in 1996, saw an opportunity to help stadium customers make better use of their time. The company created a handheld digital device connected to a local network. With such devices in place, information can be shared within the network at extremely low cost. The initial application involved saving time by allowing patrons to order food right from their handheld devices in the stadium and have it delivered to their seats.

Amaranth has since expanded aggressively into numerous arenas in which remote connectivity changes the time spent at one or more links in a customer's consumption experience. Primary client groups include restaurants, hotels, and hospitals, which use the devices to shorten the time between the customer's request and its fulfillment. Restaurants, for example, can use the software to preorder drinks and appetizers for patrons even before they have been seated. Hotels can use the technology to provide room service and speed the delivery of valet-parked cars. Hospitals can process food and medicine orders for patients faster and more precisely.

Amaranth's main product, 21st Century Restaurant software, is poised to become the industry standard for mobile wireless ordering and payment processing in restaurants. In some cases, saving time for diners also results in increased sales. Busy restaurants find that they can increase turnover by providing faster service, thus increasing the revenue they can earn per table.[4]

Example: Automating Nutritional Analysis to Save Time in Clinical Trials. Sometimes, saving time can translate into substantial cost savings. Tiny Princeton Multimedia Technologies Corporation develops software that helps nutritionists rapidly analyze patients' diets and develop better ones. The company's ProNutra software calculates and manages metabolic diet studies to eliminate paperwork and provide rapid turnaround of information. ProNutra is being used by thirty research and medical centers, including the general clinical research centers of the National Institute of Health (NIH) and USDA human nutrition research centers. Other clients include Stanford, Yale, Harvard, Rockefeller University, and the University of Chicago.

Whereas many clients are using the software as part of weight management services for their customers, substantial financial returns are expected from its widespread deployment in pharmaceutical clinical trials. Because an important control variable for a clinical trial consists of monitoring patients' nutrition intake, delays in this process can end up delaying an entire trial. According to founder Rick Weiss, "When you save a day of clinical trials, you are saving the company $1 million a day."[5]

Prospecting Questions for Eliminating Time Delays

Inspect each major link in your consumption chain.

In some links, are there delays between the time demand occurs and the time delivery is completed?

Are these delays expensive, dangerous, or frustrating for customers?

Are there ways to eliminate or shorten these delays? Are there ways to compensate for them?

Are there ways you can help your customers reduce delays for their customers?

Move #5: Monopolize a Trigger Event

A final opportunity for prospecting is to identify triggers in the chain and then find a way either to monopolize them or to be the first to notice when they occur. Have your team look for mechanisms to ensure that you are appropriately positioned to influence key decision makers at trigger points.

Example: Remote Monitoring of Elevators to Prevent Problems Before They Develop. For years, early identification of potential problems has been the core of the competition in the global business of maintaining building elevators. Then companies such as Otis (in the United States) and Kone (in Europe) invested heavily in technologies to provide early warnings of events that might trigger a maintenance call. Now these companies can either prevent the problem or arrive on-site to eradicate it.

Example: Getting the Right Advisor for Golf Cleats. A manufacturer of specialized golf cleats wrestled with the problem of determining the event that triggers customers' awareness. The company's cleats were designed to improve the golfer's grip while minimizing any harm to the grass on the golf course, a distinct advantage over the metal cleats that were then standard.

The company could have approached large sporting goods retail stores, such as Sports Authority or Dick's Sporting Goods. Or it could have approached specialty stores, online providers, or catalogs. The company decided, however, to think carefully about the trigger events that might lead a golfer to switch cleats. It concluded that among likely events would be the golfer's first visit or two to a course that did not permit use of the metal cleats.

The next question was, who would be in a position to influence the prospective customer? The company decided to approach two sets of potential influencers. The first seemed obvious: golf pros at such courses. The second was far less obvious: the people who maintained the changing facilities and organized the caddies. The folks in place in a changing room or at the clubhouse have a lot of influence. The company found that these individuals had far more influence than was commonly recognized on all kinds of purchases in the multibillion golf equipment business. Access to the people who have access to the customer at a critical trigger point in the cleat-consumption experience proved essential to the launch of that business.

Example: Jiffy Lube Creates Self-awareness of Damaging Driving Behavior. Some companies are proactive in creating triggering events that might stand in their favor. The Jiffy Lube subsidiary of Pennzoil–Quaker State, for example, used research data to create a potential triggering event.

Jiffy Lube's main business is providing convenient car maintenance services, such as oil changes. Working with Harris Interactive, Jiffy Lube discovered that most consumers were unaware of how tough many of them were on their cars. Some 86 percent of the 3,345 people surveyed initially rated themselves as normal drivers, even though they readily agreed that they drove their cars in the following ways: taking short trips, starting and driving without warm-up time, commuting in stop-and-go traffic, hauling heavy loads, pulling

---

Prospecting Questions for Monopolizing a Trigger Event

Inspect each major trigger in your consumption chain.

How can you position your offering to monopolize a trigger?

Can you be the first to know that a trigger event has occurred?

Can your firm be the first in line or first in the customer's mind when the triggering event occurs?

Can you create triggers that favor your firm or your offering?

---

a trailer, driving in extreme heat or cold, and traveling in salty, coastal areas. More than 55 percent were surprised to discover that automakers would classify these behaviors as severely damaging. Jiffy Lube's management publicized these findings during National Car Care Month, encouraging drivers to adopt more frequent maintenance procedures and thereby creating a trigger for the awareness link in the chain and hopefully increasing demand for the company's maintenance services.

Action Steps for Transforming the Customer's Experience

The action steps that follow are meant to get you started on the concepts and processes discussed in this chapter. Feel free to elaborate or adapt them in a way that works best for your company.

Step 1: Identify your most critical customer segments. For each one, sketch out the primary links in its consumption chain. Get the information by interviewing as many people in your firm as possible who are directly in contact with customers. Ideally, also work directly with a sample of customers in each segment so that you get a visceral understanding of their needs.

Step 2: Identify the trigger events that precipitate customer movement from link to link (awareness, search, selection, and so on). Articulate how your organization identifies (or could identify) when a trigger event occurs.

Step 3: Consider the procedures you would need to alert you when the trigger is activated, and develop action plans to respond.

Step 4: Assemble a multifunctional team comprising all functions in your firm that interact with the customer in any way, and take the team members through the consumption chain. Try to identify any "quick hits" that would improve the chain for your customers and improve profits for you. Remember, if you make your customer's experience at each link only a little better than that of the competition, it can be hard for customers to spot what you're doing.

Step 5: Create a group to assess the potential for making a marketbusting move using the prospecting questions and the examples in this chapter. Make a rough assessment of the gains this move might provide you and how long the advantage would last.

Step 6: Consider the most promising of the ideas as you develop your strategy for the next round of competition.

3

TRANSFORM YOUR OFFERINGS AND THEIR ATTRIBUTES

I N CHAPTER 2, we encouraged you to try to get into your customers' point of view in order to understand the experiential context in which they consume your products or services. In this chapter, you'll look through a different lens to discover what your offerings really mean to your customers.

The critical question is how the attributes (features or characteristics) of your offerings are positioned relative to your customers' view of other offerings and to your customers' expectations. It's as if you're charting your position on a map, because essentially you are trying to develop insight about your relative position.

The tool we use to get at this insight is what we call an *attribute map*. Attribute mapping simplifies the complexity of your proposition to your customers and your position with respect to competitors. In this way, attribute mapping lets you clearly see how a move might have an impact and also gives you objective information about the likely consequences of a move.[1]

Let's begin with the bad news. There will always be things about your offering that some customer segments dislike. Further, a lot of what you take time and effort to deliver is either not visible to the customer or not a factor that differentiates your product or service from the competition. Finally, the whole process of creating value for customers is dynamic: Yesterday's major differentiators become tomorrow's taken-for-granted attributes. Not fair. Not nice. But that's how it goes in open, competitive markets.

The good news is that by developing a fine-grained view of how specific segments react to specific attributes, you can develop offerings that maximize the value customers perceive, while optimizing your investment. The idea is not to offer attributes that cost you money to create but which customers don't value; you *do* want to seek those rare attributes that can make a huge competitive difference, even if they aren't that expensive. An attribute map, shown in table 3-1, gives you a tool that helps you understand and respond to your customers' real needs and desires.

An attribute map describes your offering in terms of what it does to please, or displease, key customer segments. Along the rows are the reactions of a target customer segment to the features in your product or service. The top row shows those features and attributes that customers regard positively; these attributes might prompt them to purchase and stay loyal to your products and services. The features in the second row are the negatives; these are things that customers dislike and would prefer to do without. In the third row are attributes about which customers are neutral. They don't care, or don't know, about these features.

TABLE 3-1

The Attribute Map

	Basic	Discriminators	Energizers
Positive	Nonnegotiables	Differentiators	Exciters
Negative	Tolerables	Dissatisfiers	Enragers Terrifiers Disgusters
Neutral	So-whats	Parallel differentiators	No such beast

The labels of the columns try to capture how your offering stacks up relative to other ways customers might meet their needs. If customers judge that a feature is basic, it means that they take it for granted that all competing products have that feature. The middle column lists discriminating features—those attributes that cause customers to judge one offering to be superior or inferior to another. The third column shows energizing features. These are attributes that, as far as customers are concerned, dominate the decision to buy and use the product or to contract for the service. They typically evoke a powerful emotional response that can overwhelm everything else you do.

Positive Features

A positive feature that is regarded as basic is one that the target segment expects to receive. We call these *nonnegotiables*. You need to be realistic about nonnegotiables; although you may spend enormous amounts of time and energy on them, as far as the customer is concerned they are taken for granted. Not having this basic characteristic means that this segment will simply not buy from you. Having this feature does not mean that people buy any more, pay any more, or value what you do any more. The frustrating thing about the nonnegotiable category is that it tends to be where companies spend the bulk of their time, investment, and infrastructure, but sadly, most of that effort is taken completely for granted by their target segments.

In the middle category of the top row in table 3-1 are *differentiators*. These are attributes that distinguish your offering from competitors' in a positive way and give you a favorable competitive position. (Similarly, your competitors' differentiators are what attract their customer segments to their offerings and not to yours.) Having differentiating features is great, and it can form the basis for competitively differentiated pricing and positioning.

Even more powerful are a class of attributes we call *exciter* features. Exciters are so overwhelmingly attractive to a particular customer segment that they not only distinguish you from competitors but also so delight the customer that they can constitute the basis for buying and using your offering. Exciter features plant the seeds of considerable competitive advantage.

Fascinating misconceptions abound regarding exciter features. Managers tend to believe that there is a correlation between the expense and difficulty of including a feature and the resulting excitement on the part of customers. Often this is simply not so. Exciters can be, and often are, technically simple changes that add to the convenience or ease of using the product. Hewlett-Packard, for example, is currently receiving rave reviews for designing ink-jet printers that not only produce high-quality printed photographs (a nonnegotiable) but also use photo memory cards from many manufacturers directly as inputs, thereby eliminating the need to use a computer and greatly enhancing the ease of use of the printers.

Incorporating exciter features can help you overcome drawbacks in your offering. The original success of the PalmPilot handheld device has often been attributed to its ability to overcome the weight and size limitations that plagued previous personal digital assistant (PDA) devices, although admittedly its display was not very attractive and having to learn its Graffiti writing method was awkward for many customer segments.

Negative Attributes

All products have negative attributes, so it's important to be explicit about them. First come *tolerables*. These are attributes that customers put up with to get the positives you offer. As with nonnegotiables, customers assume that tolerables come with the product and that buying from a competitor will not eliminate them.

When you think about it, most industries have many tolerables. Airlines require you to suffer security searches. Credit card companies charge interest on revolving debt. American movie theaters have sticky floors and smell like popcorn. At a minimum, all companies want you to pay for what they provide when—let's face it— we'd all rather get what is being offered for free.

The key issue here is that if a competitor can figure out how to eliminate tolerables when you still force them on customers, you can suddenly find yourself at a competitive disadvantage. A great many entrepreneurs have enjoyed big wins by recognizing attributes that customers simply tolerate because no one has yet invented a better way to remove the problem attribute at an acceptable cost. If you invent a way around tolerables, the whole product value equation can change.

When customers believe that a negative attribute of your offering could be avoided by buying a competitive offering, it becomes a *dissatisfier*. Dissatisfier features differentiate you from competitors, but in the wrong direction. Thus, cars that are perceived to require excessive service, fees perceived to be too high, technical departments thought of as unresponsive, and the like can all drive your customers away.

Even more deadly to your competitive position is a class of attributes that are energizing but negative. We call these *enragers*, although they may inspire many negative emotions, ranging from anger to fear to disgust. Obviously these features are never the result of a conscious decision; rather, they emerge as the result of misjudgment or even outright misfortune. When Monsanto attempted to launch genetically modified agricultural products in Europe, the company seriously underestimated the negative emotions such products would engender. As it turns out, Europeans are far more aware than their American counterparts of issues surrounding genetic modification, and a vocal, emotional constituency mobilized almost instantly to oppose the launch. Interestingly, it turns out that American consumers, whom Monsanto executives assumed accepted genetically modified foods, are spectacularly unaware of how many of these products they actually consume.

If you are unfortunate enough that an attribute becomes an enrager, a terrifier, or a disguster, it is critical to eliminate it before it busts *your* market. The reputation of once-dominant Perrier, for example, was so sullied by a highly publicized case of contamination that Perrier has never recovered its former market share. If you cannot eliminate an enrager, you may have to exit the enraged target market.

Negatives are a rich source of marketbusting opportunities, particularly because many firms tend to focus all their attention on working the positive line. Adding value, creating more features, and bulking up the product with enhancements all seem to be popular, but they overlook opportunities created by negatives. Apple Computer's "switch" campaign, for example, is targeted at customer segments who are enraged by the unreliable performance and lack of usability of their "Wintel" computers. Apple is betting that there is a large group of customers who might be willing to pay more and endure the negative of a conversion hassle to own a computer that doesn't crash, boots up quickly, and handles routine chores with aplomb. The devices look good, too.

If you want to gain great insights into negatives as your customers see them, the best source is to talk to the people who come into direct contact with customers or distributors. Sales, service, complaint handling, returns processing, call center, and accounts receivable staff are all likely to be exposed to customers who experience your offering, often in its worst possible light.

Neutral Attributes

Target customer segments are indifferent to neutral attributes, so in general they are not sources of marketbusting ideas. However, products can have features that are neutral from the perspective of one customer set but are basic or differentiating for a different customer set. Because neutral attributes add cost without enhancing value, one major marketbusting opportunity is to ruthlessly eliminate the culprits and thereby drive down cost and hence price. Be careful, though; for some customers, things you might think are neutral are actually nonnegotiable. For example, replacing a live person with a voice-mail system may be perfectly fine under some circumstances and deeply upsetting to customers in others.

Parallel Differentiators

Parallel differentiators are the features mapped in table 3-1 as neutral. These features have nothing to do with the functionality of the product or service as such but are offered in parallel with your offering and actually induce the purchase. For years, McDonald's has differentiated its fast-food offerings for families by offering a children's meal. Called a Happy Meal, it comes in a special box—often imprinted with entertaining games—and includes a toy. Children's meals give families a reason to choose McDonald's over other potential providers of quick food, although when you think about it they aren't really a necessary part of the food consumption experience. McDonald's has recently added grown-up happy meals to their product offerings—extending the insights gained through serving families with children. We like to include such parallel features in a strategic analysis because often they are overlooked.

Applying Attribute Maps

An even better way to systematically identify opportunities for differentiation for your different customer segments is to conduct attribute mapping of the most important consumption chain links. Make sure that you are aware of which attributes fall into which categories for key customer segments at each link in the chain, because you can then begin to ask questions such as these:

How can you deliver the positive attributes faster, better, and more cheaply and more conveniently than you do now?

How might you reduce or remove negative and neutral attributes?

How can you meet new needs that customers may be developing?

What might customers find attractive if you alone could give it to them?

The answers to each of these questions will give you a sense of the opportunities you have to move from the attribute maps created today to the marketbusting offerings that can drive profitability tomorrow.

Possibly the most important way to use an attribute map is to anticipate the dynamics of change in what customers will value and what competitors will respond to. Yesterday's exciters? Tomorrow's nonnegotiables. Yesterday's tolerables? Tomorrow's enragers. Yesterday's so-whats can easily be tomorrow's tolerables, particularly if they add cost or complexity for the customer and yet add little value. When an exciter becomes a nonnegotiable, you really want to be in a low-cost position. Many people forget this, in the joy of discovering something customers really value and will pay for. Remember, competitors won't let you keep your exciter features to yourself if they can possibly find a way to match you. Why? Because for the period when you have sole control over an exciter feature, you are creating an ever-more-powerful ability to compete, a major disadvantage for them.

Missing the Obvious

It is easy for companies to offer innovations that are not sufficiently meaningful to induce customers to change their purchasing behavior. For example, dozens of credit card companies fill the mailboxes of the affluent on a daily basis, offering low-interest or no-interest cards and the opportunity to combine balances. For this group of consumers, who typically don't run balances and don't care about the interest rate, the offered change in consumption experience creates no value. In contrast, when credit cards were first made available to students without requiring parental cosignature, it created a substantially different customer experience, with the result that student uptake was enormous. In the case of student cards, competitors of firms such as Citibank initially were not inclined to match the offer because they didn't understand how to accurately price the risk of offering cards to students.

A second mistake is to forget to design a profit capture mechanism before you introduce an innovative move. This was perhaps the largest problem facing many dot-com companies. Their management teams failed to recognize that creating value from information goods is entirely different from being paid for value created. Management in a host of failed dot-coms, such as the ill-fated Value America.com, thought simply that offering a new channel would alter customers' experiences and take share from existing players, but the model that would generate huge profits never fell into place.

A third common error is to fail to focus the segmentation effort finely enough that offerings can be fine-tuned for those groups who value them the most. Consumption chains are different for different segments, and therefore changing them will have different value for different segments. Often, companies try to alter the consumption chain for everyone they might conceivably do business with, without thinking through which segments will really be excited by the offer. Time Warner's failed "full service network" venture, for example, was based on the assumption that interactive television would be of interest to its entire customer base, most of whom (the company thought) would leap at the chance to order movies and shop interactively through their television cable systems. The company eventually lost more than $5 billion on the venture.[2]

A further mistake many companies unfortunately make is to fail to anticipate competitive responses to their moves, thus creating no vehicle for protecting their profits from competition. Competitors can learn from you about how to improve the consumption experience for their customers, often destroying your advantage. The history of discount stores, for example, shows a consistent pattern of progress in which pioneers' innovations were superceded by later entrants. Innovations pioneered by Woolworth were improved upon by operations such as Kmart, Best, Inc., and Caldor. Eventually the whole sector came to be dominated by Wal-Mart (whose premise is "everyday low prices"), leading to large-scale closures among previously successful competitors. Without some way of isolating your profits from competitors or competing in a way they find difficult to match, you can guarantee they will come after your profits.

Projecting Your Profit from a Move

In textbooks, there is no shortage of analytical techniques for assessing how likely you are to benefit from an investment in improving some aspect of your offering. In reality, we find that managers often either won't or can't take advantage of the advice in textbooks because they are not forced to take a candid, hard-nosed look at how their offerings stack up in reality.

We often see a tendency to gloss over who the competitors are to begin with. It is common to sit in on strategy debates and observe that the discussion never goes beyond the traditional competitors or sticks to such a generic view of competing offerings that it can't be a focus for action. The offerings of possible competitors are dismissed because they are assumed to be inferior in customers' eyes on some dimension such as quality or comprehensiveness. But before you feel secure, it's a good idea to check whether customers really want all that quality and comprehensiveness.

Second, companies often underestimate how rapidly competitors might respond to a move. One insurance company we worked with was furious that competitors responded to a proposed new product with the launch (soon after) of a look-alike product, which evidently was a straight copy of the original. Worse, because the copycat company didn't have to invest in market research and development, it was offering the product at more favorable rates than the innovators.

Third, it is important to remember that not all people running companies are trained as entrepreneurs or business strategists. They can sometimes overlook business basics, such as remembering to ask how a particular advantage will be sustained.

And finally, there is a widespread misconception that customers' response to a change in an offering will somehow be proportionate either to their overall levels of satisfaction with the change or to the effort and expense the company went through to offer it. Instead, marketing research suggests that customer responses to whatever a company does tend to be curvilinear: Some moves evoke a powerful, behavior-changing response, whereas others create a far more muted reaction.

A Sample Attribute Map: Home Internet Access

We thought it might be fun to illustrate attribute mapping by selecting a product category that is currently driving one of us completely crazy—namely, access to the Internet at home. As of this writing, there are not a great many alternatives in the United States for home access to the Internet. Offerings fall basically into three categories: (1) access through telephone lines; (2) access through high-speed channels, such as cable, ISDN, or DSL lines often hooked to a local area network; and (3) access through wireless devices on a mobile data network.

To start this example, we need to consider segments. In the case of your authors, Rita uses her Internet connection for research— locating examples, teaching materials, and references from various online databases. For these applications, speed and reliability are key attributes. Slow connection speed has a dramatic and immediate effect on productivity. Excite@Home, the local cable company that served Rita's home area, advertised "blazing fast speed" and actually delivered on this promise when she hooked up to the service. But when Comcast cable took over after Excite's spectacular bankruptcy, the speed of Rita's Internet connection fell off dramatically, creating frustration on her part (and on the part of everyone in her family who listened to all the complaining!).

Interestingly, Rita falls into a different segment for Comcast's purposes than someone who is converting to cable from a dial-up connection. For a former dial-up-only customer, the speed is probably an improvement. For someone used to the fast access speed of the previous system, however, the speed provided was frustratingly slow.

What would this example look like in an attribute map? Let's try mapping a few of the following features for Rita that are featured in Comcast's advertising:

- Always-on access, no dial-up

- "Comcast at home" sign-on screens

- Speed of service (transmission, download, and upload speed)

- Personalized log-on screens

- Access to proprietary content

- Comcast e-mail address, Web pages, and "my file locker" feature

- Price: $49 per month

These attributes are shown in the attribute map in table 3-2.

For Rita, who has an e-mail address provided by Columbia Business School, together with a Web site and other file storage features, the e-mail and file features of Comcast are neutrals—she simply doesn't care. But for other Comcast segments, these features are

TABLE 3-2

Attribute Map for Rita's Broadband Features

	Basic	Discriminating	Energizing
Positive	Nonnegotiable Always on, no dialing	Differentiating Still faster than dial-up	Exciting

Negative	Tolerable
	Price of $49
		Dissatisfying
		Pop-up ads
		Pop-up requests to
		   download updates
			Enraging
			Noticeably slower
			   speed than
			   previous service

Neutral	So what? Comcast sign-on screens Access to content E-mail, Web, and "my file locker" features	Parallel differentiator	

probably extremely important. Connection speed, however, is so important to segments such as Rita's that if Comcast were faced with any real competition, Rita would have been highly likely to switch providers.

Further, because Rita's segment uses the service for work purposes, price is less important than is speed. Other characteristics of the service—such as pop-up ads that request that users download software they neither need nor understand—can add to the dissatisfiers in the map. For example, this morning Rita had to deal with an irritating pop-up inviting her to download some sort of video playing software. Her reaction? "What is that? Why do I want it?"

If one were strategizing for Comcast, maps such as this one suggest issues that deserve attention. The monopolistic nature of cable service offers the company some breathing room. However, dissatisfaction with the service might easily lead Comcast to lose customer segments such as Rita's when an alternative becomes available—even at a higher price. The company could flag other alternatives, such as differentiating on price (perhaps having speed-conscious segments pay more). Each segment would be uniquely influenced by Comcast's choices. Finally, Comcast would need to be extremely careful in the event that enough customers become enraged to push for a challenge to its monopoly position.

It is only fair to say that after about six months of what appeared to be teething problems in digesting the Excite@Home acquisition, Comcast's service is once again back to acceptable levels and has been quite reliable, and Rita is once more a loyal customer. Now, if it could just do something about all that spam and adware . . .

MarketBuster Prospecting

The point of attribute mapping is to create a framework for thinking about changes you might make to your offerings for a targeted set of customers. Being conscientious about such mapping also leads you to confront competition and clearly define various segments. It can also give you early warnings about competitors' moves and motivations.

Searching for potential marketbusting moves can be a simple matter of picking up a few key attributes for certain key segments. It can also, if needed, involve a fair amount of detailed work to help you understand what is driving the consumption experiences of your customers and how your offering fits into those experiences. At the extreme, you would go back to the consumption chain you developed for your offering and, for each key segment, construct an attribute map for each link in the chain. But seldom is this amount of detailed work necessary. Instead, you can begin by mapping two or three of the most important links, such as the usage link, the purchase link, and the selection link. It is also important to recall that your specific offering may have peculiarities that require special handling. For example, if your main business is repairing elevators, your customers really don't want to see you in their buildings during rush hour.

Here are seven moves companies have used to shift the attribute maps for their offerings and create marketbusters (we'll continue the numbering from chapter 2 to make it easier for you to find a move that interests you):

Move #6: Dramatically improve positives

Move #7: Eliminate tolerables or emerging dissatisfiers

Move #8: Break up existing segments

Move #9: Infuse the offering with empathy

Move #10: Add a compelling parallel offering

Move #11: Eliminate complexity

Move #12: Capture the value you deliver

One of the beauties of attribute map moves is that often you can combine them to make an offering even more compelling. For example, if you can improve positive attributes and add a parallel offering, the move has even more potential to be a winner. In several of the examples we describe, you'll notice that companies changed their customers' attribute maps along several dimensions, not just one.

Move #6: Dramatically Improve Positives

An obvious place to look for a new potential marketbuster is to consider how you might dramatically enhance your offerings by adding powerful new differentiators or, particularly, by adding exciters. Most managers we work with enjoy thinking of ways they can better serve, please, and appeal to customers. Most ideas, however, represent opportunities that competitors will find difficult to follow quickly or be reluctant to adopt quickly. A quickly copied addition does nothing more than raise the cost of doing business.

Example: Procter & Gamble Makes Electric Toothbrushes Massively More Affordable. An interesting example of a dramatically changed offering is Procter & Gamble's latest twist on the common toothbrush—the SpinBrush. Powered by a tiny battery, the SpinBrush is an inexpensive electric toothbrush with a rotating head. Invented by three entrepreneurs and sold to Procter & Gamble, the SpinBrush put an attribute—a moving brush head—into the market at a price point that is competitive with high-end manual brushes.[3] The result was a product that dramatically changed the world of brushing, or at least of toothbrush marketing. As of this writing, it is sold in 35 countries, has contributed $200 million in global sales, and has forced competitors into an uncomfortable reactive position involving discounts on their previously higher-priced products. In the first quarter of 2003, the sales of the Crest franchise—led by new products Whitestrips and Spin-Brush—rose 30 percent and were expected to grow healthily throughout 2003.

Example: Enterprise Rent-A-Car Leases Cars to Businesses First, Consumers Second. As its name suggests, Enterprise Rent-A-Car started in the primarily business-to-business (B2B) target segment. It delivered an attribute to replace one that was temporarily unavailable: specializing in car leases to firms, such as insurance companies, that needed replacement cars while owners waited for their damaged cars to be repaired. From these beginnings the firm has grown from car rental to fleet rental to one of the largest vehicle leasing and car rental companies in North America, with revenues of $6.9 billion.

Example: Intel Expands the Mobility Attributes of Personal Computers. The introduction of Intel's Centrino mobile technology delivers new notebook computer capabilities designed specifically for the mobile world. Now it is possible to work, connect, and play without wires, as well as to choose from a new generation of thin, light notebook computers designed to enable extended battery life. Although the apparent target may be the individual customer, the bulk of Centrino sales are to firms whose high-value, highly mobile employees need to be connected as seamlessly as possible to their professional environments. The Intel Centrino brand also ensures that you don't need to study a technical manual or use special equipment to connect. That's because Intel worked with hardware and software developers and wireless service providers with the goal of delivering an integrated wireless mobile computing experience. Laptop computers equipped with the technology come with wireless connectivity and extended battery life—a compelling differentiator for professional people on the move.

Example: Ricoh Manages Total Printing Output for Customers. In Japan, Ricoh has aggressively added major positive attributes to its offering over the past twenty years. Starting as a provider of sensitized paper, Ricoh moved early into digitization and progressed from printing equipment to printing solutions—that is, total management of printing output. Now Ricoh has added a new set of positive attributes: document solutions. This offering lets users completely digitize and store documents, photos, images, data, and other types of input. For document-driven businesses,

Prospecting Questions for Improving Positives

Differentiators

To determine your offering's positive differentiators, have your customers from the key segment answer the following questions:

Why do they buy from you and not the competition?

What do you offer that they not only like but also are prepared to pay a premium for?

What does your offering do better than anyone else's?

How close is the competition to matching you on these features? Are you progressively reducing the cost of providing these features?

Exciters

Have your customers from the key segment complete the following sentences:

I would buy (or pay) more if, when I use it, I could . . .

I would buy (or pay) more if, when I buy it, I could . . .

I would buy (or pay) more if, when I select it, I could . . .

document solutions allow for flexibility of output production, including conversion of black and white to color. This strategy maximizes the propensity of customers to use Ricoh consumables such as quality papers and colored inks and gels (which have many user-friendly properties that ink lacks).

Move #7: Eliminate Tolerables or Emerging Dissatisfiers

Often, rather than add new positives, it's more powerful to find a way to eliminate tolerables or dissatisfiers. This move creates a positive for you while simultaneously creating a possible dissatisfier for your competition.

Example: The "Run Flat" PAX Tire. An interesting example is the Pax "run-flat" tire introduced by France's Michelin Group. The run-flat tire contains technology (invented in part by DuPont) that permits a driver to travel fifty or more miles after a tire sustains damage. This tire technology eliminates several drawbacks, in particular the need for drivers to stop and either change the tire or wait for roadside assistance when a puncture occurs. An additional benefit is that the tire is so reliable that it eliminates the need to transport a heavy spare tire, with a concomitant saving of fuel cost, weight, and space. Among the negatives of this offering are that it requires redesign of the car chassis and some other elements. It remains to be seen whether the "run flat" concept is powerful enough to overcome these negatives.

Example: Sweeter Smelling Stables. At the more entrepreneurial end of the spectrum is a move made by a relatively small operation, a hunter/jumper equestrian center known as Canterbury Tails in the Princeton, New Jersey, area. The business was begun by horse enthusiasts Elissa and Larry DiPano, who decided to enter the market for boarding and training show horses, which in the United States alone involves some 5.5 million horses at prices in the hundreds of dollars per month. In 1996, the pair started working on their dream by focusing on the negative attributes of existing offerings. One negative they identified was smell. Most stables, they found, were constructed with ventilation flowing up and down a center isle, meaning that when any inhabitant urinated, the air in the whole stable was perfumed. To eliminate this negative, the entrepreneurs built a facility with cross-ventilating windows in the stalls. They also addressed other major negatives in competitive offerings. The business opened its doors in 1998 and now is in the black, offering boarding and lessons in a uniquely customer-friendly environment for the horsey set. Moreover, some see the stable as a leading provider with potentially marketbusting consequences at a national level. Witness the following observation, reprinted from a local newspaper:

> *John Reiley, supervisor of operations, has his own prediction. Between heaving bales of hay into the stalls, he puffs, "I've worked 'em all—Belmont, Monmouth, Hialeah, and scores of private stables. And I tell you one thing—this is the best run outfit I've ever seen. They've made it a goldmine. Ten years from now? Hell, they'll have to beat customers away with a stick."*[4]

Example: An Appeal to Security in Flying. Discount air carrier JetBlue has made an effort to add to the emotional content of its marketing message. After the terrorist attacks of 2001, reassurance of safety became an increasingly significant customer requirement. JetBlue was the first national carrier to install bulletproof, deadbolted cockpit doors on all its aircraft. Although this safety measure may well be required by the Federal Aviation Administration in the near future, JetBlue is trying to act in advance to show that its main focus is on safety and meeting its customers' needs and wants. At the time of this writing, JetBlue is also the only airline that has implemented a full bag-matching policy (matching all checked bags to passengers on board its domestic flights) to further increase security. These processes serve to reassure customers who are deeply fearful of plane security.

Example: Providing Supplies to Individual Small Medical Practices. PSS World Medical (originally Physician Sales and Services) provides supplies to medical practices, focusing its attention on private practices; the idea is that the doctor, dentist, or other provider needs and is willing to pay handsomely for personalized attention, updated product information, and similar service needs. Among other features of the service are no shipping costs; even though orders are small, they have a high margin. With revenues of more than $1 billion, PSS serves more than one hundred thousand practices.

Prospecting Questions for
Eliminating Tolerables and Dissatisfiers

Tolerables

What are the features that your most important segments would list if you asked them to complete the following sentence: "If only you could eliminate _____ from your offering, I would buy (or pay) a lot more"?

Can you get rid of the tolerables in ways that competitors can't? How?

Are you experiencing increasing complaints about a feature or characteristic?

To what extent are your target customers beginning to compare you to your competition unfavorably with respect to this attribute?

Dissatisfiers

Which attribute do people who interact with customers hear the most grumbling about? Is it something all providers do? Is it something only you do?

Is this attribute increasingly cited as a key reason for customers returning the product or discontinuing the service?

Are any competitors claiming that they are superior with respect to this attribute?

Move #8: Break Up Existing Segments

In a disruptive resegmentation move, your goal is to break apart existing segmentation schemes by changing the attributes offered to customers. Perhaps a particular segment is underserved, or perhaps you have identified a new or emergent need that is not addressed by current offerings.

Example: Local Delivery of Office Supplies in Tokyo. Japanese office supplies firm ASKUL has focused on a much under-served B2B segment: the small office. Small to medium-sized offices in Japan have been largely ignored by major stationery stores. Before ASKUL, someone had to be dispatched to the local small stationery store, where urgently required items often were not in inventory. ASKUL developed a sophisticated distribution network organizing these local stationery stores to deliver office supplies the next day (ASKUL means "comes tomorrow"). Now if you call, fax, or e-mail in the morning, the items will be delivered the same afternoon. This saves our colleague Ichiro Suzuki at T. Ohe & Associates, for example, a good sum of money because he no longer has to pay someone an hourly wage plus transportation costs to get urgent office supplies. Even larger regional offices are starting to use this service because it saves the several days it typically takes to get an order delivered.

Example: Leapfrog the Establishment. A powerful form of resegmentation involves leveraging insights into buyer behavior or changing buyer behavior to create a favorable segment. This approach was taken by upstart Econet Wireless International, a private firm founded by Zimbabwean entrepreneur Strive Masiyiwa. Econet's goal was to become a major force in Pan-African telecommunications, in direct competition with the Ministry of Posts and Telecommunications, which runs the state-owned Posts and Telecommunications Company (PTC). Originally, the PTC denied Strive Masiyiwa a cellular license. Masiyiwa hired a team of lawyers and, after five years, won the right to compete for cellular customers on December 31, 1997. Ironically, the very inefficiency of the PTC created a receptive market for a more efficient service based on the GSM global standard, even for those customers with a landline installed. Econet's strategy focused on eliminating the negatives with respect to government offerings and creating positives, such as affordable and reliable cell phone service that could be obtained quickly.

Masiyiwa focused his marketing efforts directly on the deficiencies of the state-run system. He sought to change the behavior of existing PTC customers and, more importantly, to offer an alternative to those who were not yet telecommunications users. Econet's initial target customers were opinion leaders and academics who would create a sense of legitimacy for Zimbabwe's first private telecommunications offering. Against a background of notoriously inefficient government operations, Econet presented itself as a company that was standing up to a corrupt government system. The entrenched ZANU PF party had been losing the support of the urban population because of its failure to halt the rapid decline of the Zimbabwean economy. State-run enterprises were notorious for corruption. For many customers, using the Econet service was viewed as making a political statement against corruption and supporting the success of an enterprising fellow Zimbabwean.

Political philosophy aside, Econet still faced the problem that many potential users were resource-constrained and would be leery of agreeing to use potentially expensive cellular phones. The company therefore developed a wide range of options tailored to the needs of customers having differing capabilities to afford services. The flagship offering is a service called "Buddie Pay as You Go," a prepaid cellular plan with airtime bought by the user in advance. The main marketing message is that this is a way to control one's budget, an important feature in a volatile economic climate (2001 inflation, for example, is estimated to be 300 percent). The company has also tailored packages to cater to various behavioral patterns of cell phone use, by offering the three contract packages shown in table 3-3.

In addition, Econet pioneered value-added services (for an additional fee). These include EcoFax (a fax message forwarding service), Ecomail (a personal answering service), Executive Briefing (a news access service), News on Demand (news content broadcast through the cellular phone), Eco-Note (a short message service), Roaming (for travelers), and a Crisis Center offering that makes rapid linkages to emergency service providers.

From its founding on September 10, 1998, Econet's market share has expanded to 48 percent of Zimbabwe's mobile operator market

TABLE 3-3

Econet Contract Packages

Amount of airtime required	Low	Occasional	High
Contract type	Consumer	Liberty	Business/Excel
Target demographic	Mature domestic household	Younger domestic household	Businessperson/ Executive

(one hundred thirty thousand subscribers). Econet is now moving rapidly into Kenya, Nigeria, Malta, Lesotho, and Botswana, with the objective of becoming a Pan-African telecom operator. It currently is the third largest.

Example: Leveraging Interest in Music into Retail. Retailer Hot Topic has resegmented a portion of the market for apparel, accessories, and clothing by focusing entirely on young men and women aged twelve to twenty-two who have a passion for music-licensed and music-influenced clothing and other items. Demand for Hot Topic merchandise has been fueled by the popularity of music videos on television channels such as MTV and the ubiquitous marketing efforts of popular artists. The company opened its first store in 1989 in California and operated 274 stores as of February 3, 2001, in forty-five states across the United States. Its slogan "Everything about the music" suggests a differentiated position that the company has been able to maintain, even in the face of intense, mall-based competition seeking to serve the teenage segment. We guess that most readers of this book will not be up on the latest in such products as navel rings styled to resemble those of the wearer's favorite singer, but you heard it from us: The segment is large and is willing to spend money. In 2003, Hot Topic stores attracted enough shoppers to turn in $443 million in sales.

Hot Topic offers an amazing variety of goods—some ten thousand stockkeeping units' (SKUs) worth, all with a music-oriented

---

Prospecting Questions for Breaking Up Existing Segments

Underserved Segments

Is there any current or emerging segment that is being underserved by the current attribute maps for major links in the consumption chain?

Are there trends that might give you the opportunity to break apart an existing segment?

Behavioral Segmentation

Have you looked at how various people behave at various links in the chain?

Can you segment by creating a set of attributes that will appeal to the need that customers are seeking to address at the moment that behavior becomes important?

Have you considered common behaviors that cut across demographic segments—for instance, when some customers simply want to be taken care of with little fuss while others prefer a more personal touch?

---

theme. For a retail company, Hot Topic's financial track record has been extremely strong. The company first sold stock to the public in 1996 and today has a market value approaching $400 million.

Move # 9: Infuse the Offering with Empathy

We work with a fair number of companies that are heavily populated by engineers, scientists, and trained analysts. It never fails to intrigue us how often our superrational colleagues are surprised by the success of an offering that doesn't perform better or cost less but is kinder, funnier, or more meaningful than competitive offerings. One powerful place to start looking for a marketbusting chance is therefore to consider ways that you can enhance a customer's experience. You can either add attributes that make your offerings nicer and kinder or remove those that make it hostile and unfriendly.

Example: Eco-friendly Reusable Packaging. Japan-based Starway Inc. developed environmentally friendly reusable packaging for office equipment such as computers and printers and further streamlined the process of transporting the equipment by offering pickup and delivery services. Seiko Epson used Starway's service and cut package costs and pickup and delivery fees by 50 percent. Companies such as Epson Direct use this service in their repair operations. Customers call Seiko Epson for repair services, and Seiko Epson in turn calls Starway to pick up the printer and package it for transportation. The truck operator quickly puts the printer into Starway's reusable package and brings it to Seiko Epson's repair office. After the repair is completed, the truck is again dispatched to pick up the repaired printer and deliver it to the customer in the reusable package. At the customer site, the driver opens the package and installs the repaired printer. The driver then returns the reusable package to Starway. Seiko Epson pays for using Starway's system and still saves 50 percent over the cost of the previous approach, which involved single-use packaging and a variety of logistics providers. The customer benefits because there is no need to dispose of the package. Seiko Epson (and other electronics manufacturers) wins, Starway wins, the customer wins, and the environment wins.

Example: Adding a Touch of Humor to a Serious Subject. Another of our favorites is the legal service company behind the Web site www.expertlaw.com. In addition to referrals to private investigators and expert witnesses, this firm provides a catalog of lawyer jokes under a heading called "legal humor." Here's an example:

Q: What's wrong with lawyer jokes?

A: Lawyers don't think they're funny, and other people don't think they're jokes!

What we found interesting about this example is that if you search on the Web for the phrase "legal humor," you fairly quickly unearth www.expertlaw.com, providing the firm an inexpensive bit of potential awareness building and a point of differentiation from many other Web sites that offer the same services.

Example: Videos for the Smarter Baby. Looking for opportunities to make your offerings more empathic is a good time to start watching for those experiences that customers find frustrating, alienating, or even frightening, or to take note of those they find cool, interesting, or useful. One entrepreneurial idea we found appealing along these lines is a company called Baby Einstein, which produces videos for babies. The company founder, new mother Julie Clark, invented the concept when looking for a way to introduce her children to music and art at a very young age. Together with her husband, multiple-venture entrepreneur Bill Clark, she founded the business—which five years later was sold to the Disney organization for a reputed $25 million—with an initial working capital of $5,000.

The videos themselves are very basic, with black and white backgrounds, full-screen images, and simple, short material—for instance, variations on classical music played one note at a time or cartoonlike images of famous paintings. The Clarks' understanding of what would appeal to babies also appealed to parents, who greatly enjoyed watching their offspring quietly absorbing the videos rather than squirming or crying. The great success of this business depended entirely on empathy, particularly the warm feeling parents get from a combination of gaining a few uninterrupted minutes and the potential advantages of their newborns' exposure to art and culture. Even the name of the company suggests upper-middle-class striving!

Example: Trendy Clothes for the Larger Teen. Hot Topic, mentioned earlier, plans to attempt a new marketbuster by introducing a retail concept called Torrid to attend to the clothing needs of young obese women. Torrid will offer a selection of apparel, lingerie, shoes, and accessories for plus-size women between the ages of fifteen and thirty. This concept came to the attention of company management because members of the target segment persistently requested clothing in larger sizes than Hot Topic's normal range but tailored to the same sensibility that has driven Hot Topic's growth. Women in this segment felt largely ignored by existing providers, creating a resegmentation opportunity. Although there is an increasing concern with obesity as a health risk, this segment does appear to be substantial.

Example: You're a Star! EasyJet, a U.K.–based discount carrier, enjoys an unusual brand of empathic connection. In January 1999, a series titled *Airline* was transmitted on Britain's ITV, giving a "warts and all" account of life for passengers and staff at easyJet. (*Airline* was one of the very first reality shows.) By June 2000, more than 40 percent of the viewing public was tuning in to the show, which had more loyal viewers than the new version of *Friends*. Equally empathic, the easyJet Web site allows guests to select their preferred language and provides access to a variety of travel options, including access to cobranded services provided by easyCar and easyInternetcafe.

Example: Cracking the Upgrade Treadmill. Small businesses are constantly faced with the paralyzing decision of whether to upgrade their computer systems and face "upgrading obsolescence" by having next-generation systems released shortly afterward, or to hang in and run the risk of falling behind in IT technology. Direct Leasing has found an empathic solution by absorbing the obsolescence risk for firms that lease computers from it. If your current leased equipment is obsolete, Direct Leasing will help you manage the transition to the new system.

Prospecting Questions for Infusing Empathy

Adding Empathy

Can you redesign the offering at any link to make the customer experience more enjoyable?

Can you make the customer feel more satisfied, safer, more confident, less frustrated, more secure, or more amused?

Behavioral Attuning

Are the attributes you offer a good fit for the target segment's behavior?

Have you taken these customers' financial, social, and attitudinal perspectives into account when designing the offering?

Move #10: Add a Compelling Parallel Offering

Just as they often overlook changes that can make products and services nicer or friendlier, companies often overlook opportunities to differentiate their products by offering something in parallel with them. The additional offering may not do anything to the features or functions of the original offering, but it can greatly influence your customers' experience.

Example: Classical Music with a Difference. If we were to ask you to guess the name on the label that appears on five of the fourteen million-selling classical music compact discs, would you guess that the name is Victoria's Secret? Part of The Limited organization, Victoria's Secret is a purveyor of ladies' racy lingerie. Think about it: As consumers shop, the music plays, and then right there at the checkout is the CD. If one is shopping for a special occasion, why not pick up the music that would . . . uh . . . enhance the experience? Further, unlike a classical music expert, who might venture unafraid into a music megastore, lingerie shoppers can buy albums already put together by experts, with an assurance that the music will be appropriate. Interestingly, the trend toward music compilations that fit a retailer's theme has now spread to many other stores and store environments, creating a new category for music consumption: music designed to be enjoyed in parallel with other activities. Thus, Starbucks provides music for the caffeinated, Pottery Barn offers tunes appropriate for "Dinner at Eight," and Gap offers music to go with its cool clothes.

Sometimes you can differentiate even the most commoditized of products by adding a compelling parallel offering. The parallel has nothing to do with the product per se but can create the incentive to buy or to stay loyal. Airlines, hotels, bookstores, credit card companies, and even pizza stores are using a variety of twists on the frequent buyer theme to offer parallel offerings to their best customers in the hope of keeping them loyal. For airlines, a frequent flyer program can outweigh other choice criteria, such as the time and location of a flight. It's even better if the miles are going toward a family vacation, because the parallel effect multiplies as beloved partners encourage their loved ones to stay true to one provider in order to earn that last free ticket.

Example: A Purchase from Us Is a Vote Against Corruption. Econet, the Zimbabwean telecommunications company we discussed earlier, believed that a powerful parallel offering to its cellular phone service consisted of its stand against corruption. Using an Econet phone became something of a symbol of resistance and provided an interesting first-mover positioning advantage relative to the entrants now flooding into deregulated African telecom markets.

Example: Enhancing Commodities with Services. In any firm selling commodities, such as fertilizer, industrial gases, metal components, paper, and textiles, the essence of avoiding price-cutting

Prospecting Questions for Adding a Compelling Parallel Offering

Direct Customer Benefits

Is there anything that you can offer in parallel with your offering that will give you the edge in attracting customers?

Is there anything you can do to make your customers' experience better, even if it doesn't seem to relate to what you produce or do?

Indirect Customer Benefits

Is there any way your company or your offering can be associated with something the customer values?

---

death spirals lies in assembling parallel services, such as assistance with inventory planning, production planning, and process planning, or provision of financing services to reduce the cash pressure of a purchase. In fact, over time, the parallel offerings may become valuable in themselves, and you may then need to take the unpopular step of charging for them, as you will see in the next section. There are two challenges here. The first is to anticipate shifts in the needs of the customer's consumption chain and position yourself to enhance the commodity you are offering. The second lies in being able to anticipate and astutely prune any parallel offerings that are no longer needed, thereby minimizing the cost of the expanded offering.

Move # 11: Eliminate Complexity

Have you ever bought multiple generations of a product, only to find that over time so many features have been added that you are actually less satisfied with the later models than the earlier ones? If you have, you have lived through the opportunity for what we call radical surgery, a move to dramatically eliminate complexity. Radical surgery is made possible, ironically, by the very efforts of companies to be responsive and to invest in improving their offerings. Often, firms offer more and more options, functionality, and features to the point that the complexity of the offering becomes a dissatisfier. A potential marketbuster can consist of rediscovering exactly what customers want and will pay for and then ruthlessly eliminating everything that doesn't meet those two criteria. When the time is ripe for someone in the industry to do radical surgery of the offering, you act as the surgeon.

Example: Simplify, Simplify, Simplify. The proliferation of functions and features that comes with technological complexity can create a fiasco:

Last Christmas Eve, just as Lynne Bowman was preheating her oven to roast a turkey for 15 guests, her daughter accidentally brushed against one of the new oven's many digital controls. "We heard this 'beep beep beep,'" recalled Ms. Bowman, a 56-year-old freelance creative director who lives in Pescadero, Calif., "and no more oven. After that, we couldn't get it to work." Ms. Bowman's husband, an engineer, was unable to fix the problem. Nor were any of the assembled guests, half of whom were also engineers. Desperate, Ms. Bowman resorted to the small, simple 1970s-vintage Tappan electric oven in the guest house, which worked like a charm.[5]

Ironically, the digital intelligence that is supposed to make life simpler often has the opposite effect. Video recording devices have more buttons than one can count, tuning a car radio is an ordeal, televisions now require complex manipulation of remote controls, and even changing the clocks for daylight saving time twice a year can be challenging. Attributes intended to be useful, such as timer settings or environmentally sensitive automatic adjustments, can be enormously frustrating if their use is not intuitive. And some products, such as the software we are using to write this book, *do* things to your work without your asking it to, often provoking a time-consuming search for a way to undo the changes that were made!

A company that has capitalized on radical surgery is Teac, a Japanese consumer electronics company. It has developed a Nostalgia line of stereo systems that use no digital interface mechanisms at all. Instead, the retro radios feature looks from the past and have simple knobs for analog tuning. You can even hear the static between radio stations! In automobiles, cars such as the PT Cruiser elicit feelings of a less complex era. Similarly, trendy consumer retailer Hammacher Schlemmer is capitalizing on a longing for simplicity by offering record players (yes, the 33-rpm kind) that can be carried around and folded into their own cases.

Example: A Stripped-Down Hotel Experience. The quest for simplicity can also be useful in B2B services. One rapidly growing category in the hotel industry, for example, consists of hotels that provide accommodations for long-term corporate visitors, such as contract employees, people whose homes are being renovated, corporate employees, and consultants on extended assignments. An exemplary company offering services to this segment is Extended Stay America, which operates three hotel brands. The typical menu of hotel services is stripped down; there is no bar, no lounge, no central gathering area. Housekeeping is done weekly, and guests typically handle their own laundry rather than send it to a service. In exchange, guests receive "homelike" amenities such as kitchenettes with microwave ovens and refrigerators, coffeemakers, and a dining table, as well as lower prices than the full-service alternative.

Extended Stay America has enjoyed explosive growth since its founding in 1995, becoming publicly listed in 1997. It is the fastest-growing owned and operated hotel company in U.S. history, and for three years in a row it was named one of the *Fortune* magazine's one hundred fastest-growing firms. However, it has also shown competitors the way. According to the American Hotel & Motel Association (AHMA), some seventeen new extended-stay brands have entered the market in the past five years, suggesting that Extended Stay

Prospecting Questions for Eliminating Complexity

Are there attributes you could eliminate and thus reduce your cost and potentially the price to the customer?

Are customers complaining about the complexity of your products or services?

Can you readily identify features that many of your target segments don't care about?

America will be under pressure and that later entrants are likely to face a much more challenging competitive market. Even more intriguing, however, will be to watch the impact on conventional hotels as the stripped-down versions eat away at their markets.

Move #12: Capture the Value You Deliver

We often hear this complaint at seminars: "My business is a commodity! It costs me more and more to stay in business, but the pressures on prices and margins aren't giving me the payback I need. What should I do?" When we get to the bottom of what is going on, often the issue is that the company is giving away attributes that customers value, hoping to extract higher prices for traditional services. As you saw in the case of parallel offerings, many materials- or components-based suppliers give away knowledge and processes as parallels to sell materials or components, unaware that their knowledge has become the more valuable part of the equation. Similarly, some companies create enormous value for customers simply by participating in a market and thus introducing competition, and yet they fail to reap the rewards.

This brings us to the last opportunity for marketbuster prospecting we'll deal with here: moves that help you extract a price for providing attributes that you might have given away for free.

Example: If It's Valuable, You Can Charge for It. A classic example of this strategy in the business services sector was carried out years ago by an acquaintance of MacMillan's who was put in charge of Standard & Poor's (S&P) rating service. Our acquaintance realized that the bond ratings S&P was publishing for free were of enormous value to the firms being rated. Because of the S&P rating, these firms found it easier to raise capital and gain legitimacy, in some cases garnering huge advantages compared with unrated firms. The manager decided that henceforth any firm that was rated by S&P should pay an annual fee for the service.

Naturally, firms that had been receiving the rating service for free were initially outraged. Our acquaintance, however, took the position that if they didn't find value in the rating they were free not to pay the fee—and to forgo being rated. The disadvantages of not being rated far outweighed the fee being charged. This simple decision continues to create a huge profit stream for the company (and similar rating organizations) from a service that was treated as a giveaway for years.

Example: Food-Safe Carbon Dioxide. Another interesting example involves The BOC Group, a global supplier of industrial gases that is involved in a good many commodity markets. One such market is selling the kind of carbon dioxide that beverage companies use to put the fizz into soda and other carbonated beverages. With a little help from a purity scare involving a competitor's product in Belgium, customers became concerned about the sourcing and mechanics of their CO_2. BOC turned this into a competitive advantage, charging for source guarantees and purity assurance services that previously it had largely embedded in its gases offerings. In this case, customers were happy to pay the extra charges to ensure the quality of their supply.

Example: Profit from Customization in a Commodity Industry. Worthington Industries has earned the right to much higher margins in an industry traditionally plagued by thin margins—steel processing—by focusing on orders of any size, deliveries

Prospecting Questions for Capturing Value

Customer Takes Offering for Granted

Are you providing an important service or benefit to the customer but not getting paid for it?

Would the customer not buy if you started to charge?

Customer Benefits from Attributes

Can you generate revenues differently—perhaps by menu pricing?

Can you create an *annuity stream*? In other words, is there a way to charge a per-use fee or monthly fee?

with short notice, and a willingness to customize orders. Worthington has become a $2.2 billion global player, with sixty-one facilities in ten countries on five continents. It was named one of the most admired companies in *Fortune* in 2002 and 2004.

Wrapping Up

This chapter suggests that a useful way to think about your company is as a translation device between what the customer needs and what you can do. Your task is to get that translation just right so that the price you charge represents fair compensation for the value you create.

Action Steps for Transforming Your Offerings and Their Attributes

Step 1: Put together a working group of people who come into contact with your three or four most important existing or desired customer segments. Describe these segments.

Step 2: Using the group to brainstorm, develop a preliminary attribute map for the most important customer segments. If you have created the consumption chains described in chapter 2, use them as input into the maps. At first, try to get a sense of what the map looks like today, and categorize the relevant attributes.

Step 3: Validate the assumptions in your attribute map by reality-checking them with representatives of customers or customers' companies (and distributors, if appropriate). Revise the maps.

Step 4: Assemble a marketbusting team containing representatives from the most important links, and begin prospecting for marketbusting moves. Build on the discussion in this chapter to look for opportunities.

Step 5. Categorize the ideas into a table, as shown in table 3-4.

Step 6: Create a plan to tackle priority 1 ideas first and priority 2 ideas next. Evaluate the "hard to implement'" options against the other opportunities you are assessing. Remember to assess the opportunities using the DRAT table, which will be described in chapter 7.

TABLE 3-4

Prioritizing Ideas

	Potential for Huge Positive Impact	Likely to Have Modest Positive Impact
Easy to implement	1	2
Hard to implement	3	Only if you are out of other ideas

4

REDEFINE KEY METRICS

WE HAVE SO FAR FOCUSED on what you can do for one important constituency, namely, your customers. In competitive capitalist markets, however, companies have other important constituencies, one of the most important being those who provide the capital that fuels investment to begin with. The two are somewhat linked: Absent the ability to create value for customers, investors are unlikely to feel a firm has future growth potential. But creating value for customers does not necessarily imply that a firm is going to create value for its investors. Capturing, not only creating, value is essential to building a good reputation in the capital markets. In this chapter, we will explore techniques for market-busting by transforming your performance using the lens of the investor. The goal is to create advantages in your markets, but also to have a positive effect on your firm's stock market capitalization. This is the price of your shares multiplied by the number of shares outstanding, and it is a good simple measure of how the financial markets value your company (we will refer to it as market cap).

Understanding what influences the capital markets' evaluation of your company's stock is no mystery: For established industries at least, analysts and the investors they influence tend to look at a well-developed set of ratios or key numbers that tell them how you are doing relative to everybody else in your industry. Let your costs be higher, your asset utilization lower, your inventory turns less frequent, and so on, and you will pay the price in lower assessment of your future potential, often manifest in a lower price-to-earnings ratio (or P/E as it is often called) than your competitors. A low P/E makes a firm vulnerable to all sorts of risks, such as hostile takeover, because it means the company's stocks are relatively cheap.

So, what are investors looking for? Typically, growth in market cap. How do you demonstrate that you can deliver growth? We believe there are two dominant ways. First, demonstrate that you can outperform your industry on those dimensions of performance that have become well understood by doing things that are different from the competition. Second, demonstrate that you have viable new opportunities for future good performance that make your stocks a good bet—what the academic community refers to as "growth options."[1] What is the scorecard for how well you are doing on these two factors? The scorecard is the set of key metrics that investors use to determine how good you really are.

The lens of the investor relies on two closely related concepts—your firm's unit of business and the key metrics associated with this unit of business. The unit of business is what you sell. The key metrics tell observers how successful you are at selling it.

Although it isn't unusual to take your unit of business for granted, it is vitally important to recognize that the unit of business is a strategic choice. The marketbusting moves in this chapter have in common that they involve either dramatically changing a unit of business or dramatically changing the processes used to manage an existing unit.

What Is a Unit of Business?

By *unit of business*, we mean the fundamental thing that you sell. For manufacturing companies, the traditional unit of business is literally a unit, typically of a product. So companies that manufacture

CT scanners, index cards, or compressed gas cylinders charge for the number of those things that customers buy.

In services, the potential units of business are more varied. Typically, professional services firms (law firms, accountancies, consultants) charge for a unit of time, such as a billing day. Time is also the core unit of other service businesses, such as the time spent talking (for telecommunications companies), the length of a stay (for a hotel), or the length of time (for a lease or rental). As an industry develops and matures, most players settle on a common unit of business.

When everyone takes a common unit of business for granted, one route to marketbusting is to change the rules by changing the unit. GE Medical Systems, for example, changed its focus from selling medical devices to selling equipment utilization contracts. The BOC Group went from selling gas molecules to selling a variety of services—including remote plant management and on-site supply services—to its customers. Siemens Medical Systems changed from selling cures for diseases to selling total health management services, including prevention systems. Some consulting firms have moved from a payment model of the traditional retainer or hourly contract to a model that calculates payment based on value generated or even on equity appreciation in the underlying businesses of their clients.

Why is this kind of change important? Because it's hard for competitors to anticipate, and then very hard for them to match. Competitors are accustomed to anticipating your moves through the lens of an existing way of doing business. When you change your unit of business, they can sometimes entirely overlook what you're up to. For instance, it's become commonplace to blame file swapping for the woes of the music business. What has received far less airtime is the impact of readily available music in digital form on businesses such as traditional advertising-supported radio. Indeed, one recent study reported a 25 percent drop in radio-listening time by teens in Canada, coupled with substantial growth in satellite radio station subscriptions, in which people pay to listen, but don't have to put up with commercials.[2] The unit of business in the radio business is thus being redefined—from a unit based on advertising revenue to a unit having to do with the attractiveness of the content the stations provide.

Your unit of business is critically important because it affects how you go to market, how you price, whom you sell to, whom you employ, and how you plan and execute your operations. A firm selling its customers magnetic resonance imaging (MRI) equipment is run and managed very differently from a firm selling its customers MRI utilization contracts, even though both firms feature MRI machines. Different units of business can also lead to paradoxical competitive exchanges: Consider the competition between a firm that gives away software in order to sell proprietary equipment facing off against a competing firm that gives away equipment to lock in long-term software contracts. It's as if the two companies are playing completely different games, and in a sense they are, because their units of business are different. What becomes interesting in competitive exchange is that each will have built up capabilities that make it very hard to compete on the same ground as the other.

What Is a Key Metric?

A *key metric* is a measure that captures something about how many units of business you are likely to sell and how much money you will make selling them. We have found that up to 90 percent of the impact you can make on profitability and profit growth stems from managing around seven to ten critical measures. Key metrics tap the key success factors in your strategy—those few things you must get right. Some people refer to them as key performance indicators (KPIs) or critical success factors (CSFs). We really don't mind what you call them, as long as the term captures the essence of the idea: just a few numbers that explain an awful lot and that a company has to get right.

In the airline industry, for example, one huge cost component is the relatively fixed costs of purchasing and operating planes, reservation systems, and staff. How good the airline is at filling its planes also makes a difference, because unused seating capacity on a flight represents perishable revenues (and hence profits) that can never be recaptured. Consequently, two key metrics that are commonly used by airlines analysts are the fixed cost per passenger mile flown and the passenger yield (meaning the extent to which the seats on the plane are filled).

In insurance, particularly life insurance, premium revenues come in long before the bulk of expenses go out the door as claims. Most competitors earn the bulk of their profits not on their underwriting, but on the investment income that they earn after premiums are received and before losses are claimed. To the extent that few losses are claimed relative to current revenue received, the company will have more to invest in revenue-generating assets and therefore will be more profitable. To the extent that an insurance firm keeps a good handle on administrative expenses, its profits and profit prospects are enhanced. In this industry, therefore, key metrics analysts look at the loss ratio (the proportion of losses claimed to premium revenue received) and the expense ratio (the proportion of sales and general administrative expenses to premium revenue received). Together, these two key metrics form an important combined ratio that investors and analysts examine to compare the performance of one insurance company relative to another.

Retailers operating conventional bricks-and-mortar stores have only so much floor space to display and sell items. This space limitation has for years led analysts to use ratios such as same-store sales (in which sales for one time period at one store are compared to a similar previous time period) and sales per square foot (compared to the stores' previous record, to the performance of sister stores, or to competitors' stores). Increased stock turnover means that less money is tied up in working capital, the margin on the item is captured more frequently, and the company can enjoy greater velocity of sales. Thus, another key metric in traditional retail businesses is inventory turns, on an annual (or shorter) basis, meaning the number of times inventory must be restocked.

Figure 4-1 suggests an approach to linking the unit of business with just a few key metrics.

FIGURE 4-1

Associating a Unit of Business with Critical Key Metrics

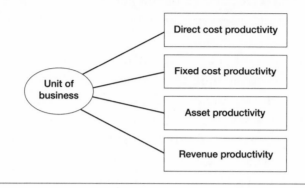

The key metrics lens for marketbusting involves doing two things: (1) either thinking of a way to dramatically improve your performance on key metrics that are already in place; or (2) changing your unit of business and developing a new set of key metrics. Sometimes the major benefit of this approach comes when you can figure out a way to improve *customers'* key metrics so that they perceive value from your activities. In both cases, improving key metrics improves your positioning with respect to your investors, ideally leading to improved assessment of your prospects and a higher market cap.

Hunting Down High-Potential Key Metrics

How to find key metrics for marketbusting? Although there is no magic recipe, generally you'll want to combine insights about your own operations, competitive intelligence, and data from publicly available sources. Here are our "top ten" places to go for the publicly available portion of the key metrics analysis.

1. *Industry benchmarks.* You'll find it easy to locate key comparative metrics for companies in mature industries, particularly

in the United States. In established industries, time and experience have created a consensus about those industry benchmarks that constitute key metrics. In other countries and for new businesses, it can be harder. For example, businesses based on the Internet are still working out appropriate key metrics. Should the model be fee-for-transaction-based? An advertising model with the infamous "eyeball counts" that characterized the Internet bubble period? Will pricing be fixed or dynamic? Will the unit of business be a standalone offering or will it reflect a combination of products and services? Although this lack of established benchmarks can be frustrating (not to mention confusing), it offers an opportunity. The firm that can shape which key metrics come to represent the way in which its industry or segment is evaluated often enjoys substantial investor appreciation—that is, provided that it follows up on its promises![3]

2. *Analyses of your own company data.* What better way to gain insight that is unique than to leverage your own experience? There are a number of useful techniques (some of which we described in chapter 6 in our earlier book) to develop trend analyses based on your own data.[4] Similarly, you can use any number of sensitivity analysis models to determine how you might create future advantage. Analyze your recent income statements and balance sheets and use sensitivity analyses to build a picture of which variables most influence your firm's profit and profit growth.

3. *Analysts' reports.* Look at the reports on your company or industry written by investment bank and stock market analysts to discover the metrics they use. Clues about the key industry profit metrics will appear in their comments about the reasons for industry profits.

4. *Bankers.* Commercial bankers who specialize in loans for your industry often develop ratios to assess the riskiness of

their loans. They also have industry-level data that you can use as benchmarks.

5. *Industry associations and industry-specialized consulting firms.* If you have an industry association, check to see whether it maintains firm- and industry-level metric data-banks. Also scan association publications for indicators. In some industries, competitors actually supply information to the association in order to facilitate comparisons. The ISO (Insurance Services Office), for instance, compiles data from insurance companies. In other industries, firms have emerged that independently collect benchmark data. Greenwich Asso-ciates, an independent company, collects and analyzes data on financial institutions and offers consulting advice. Its an-nual rankings are considered an authoritative source on the performance of financial institutions.

6. *Online databanks.* Vast amounts of data are available in on-line data services such as Value Line, Compustat, and others. The Wharton School has a user-friendly financial analysis ser-vice (WRDS) that provides access to many online databases. In addition to publications and analyst reports, many of these databases provide rankings and comparison information.

7. *Industry-specific Web sites.* Since the commercialization of the Web, any number of industry-specific sites have sprung up with the aim in part of collecting and sharing information as well as doing business. *BusinessWeek* recently reported that some $3.9 trillion in e-commerce transactions will take place in 2004.[5] You will find industry and competitive infor-mation on the World Wide Web at industry-specific sites such as e-STEEL, investment sites such as those run by E*Trade, and information-oriented sites such as Hoovers.com.

8. *The business press.* You can get insights by scanning business publications and the business section of major newspapers and periodicals, notably the *Economist*. In particular, look for

commentaries about why your current industry is cooking or in the doldrums—key clues about the industry profit drivers.

9. *Books and other publications.* You can sometimes get interesting insights by scanning the business sections of libraries and bookstores and by searching Amazon.com and Barnesand noble.com for specific industry-level publications.

10. *Government publications and NGO Web sites.* Federal and international agencies (such as the United Nations or the World Bank) often publish reports on specific industries or sectors (such as the energy or environmental sectors). Many also operate rich Web sites that provide even more information. The United Nations Statistics Division (http://unstats.un.org/unsd), for example, provides access to a vast number of demographic and industry statistics that can help you identify key trends and opportunities.

If all this seems overwhelming, you may want to consider tapping into the talent of people who have been trained to sift through lots of information to distill key insights. People with an MBA degree, for instance, have usually been marched through exercises such as the one we are proposing you undertake and are often quite skilled at data analysis and interpretation. And the good news is that they are often readily available for a reasonable price as summer interns. A "key metrics" type project would make an excellent internship opportunity both for the student and for your company.

A word of warning here that we cannot overemphasize: You do not need highly precise data; instead, you need *indicative* data. In seeking marketbusting moves you are not interested in marginally improving a key metric. Rather, you are interested in either substantially improving it or completely replacing it, so precision is relatively unimportant. What is crucial is to have convincing evidence that the metrics you are considering are in fact indicative of profits and profit growth at the firm level and the industry level.

Developing a New Unit of Business

It should be easy to determine what your unit of business is. What do you charge for? When you send customers invoices, what do you bill for? Try to spell it out in the simplest terms possible: "We make money by billing our customers or clients for _____."

When you have figured out what it is that you bill for, you have an opportunity for creativity in figuring out whether there might be a different way to generate profits by selling customers something different from what you sell today. So, if you sell a product, might you instead sell the benefits or services yielded by that product? If you sell a unit of time, might you instead see advantages in selling the results that the customer actually wants, rather than the time it took you to create them (which, quite honestly, they couldn't care less about)?

Analysts' use of key metrics presents a challenge: If you decide to change your unit of business, you will face the task of training your analysts to use metrics that are appropriate for the kind of business you seek to operate. Be aware that they will be understandably reluctant to evaluate your business in a new way, because it makes their lives much more difficult to abandon the few predictable key numbers they have used to formulate recommendations.[6]

With key metrics in hand, you can begin to think through whether you have the potential to make a marketbusting move by changing either the conventional unit of business in your industry or the way performance is measured (or, ideally, both). You can also begin to think through whether you can help customers compete more effectively by changing or improving their key metrics. Let's illustrate with the intriguing story of a cement company that radically changed its industry.

The Story of CEMEX

Selling cement is hardly the kind of business that (at least for most of us) gets the heart racing at the prospect of heady growth potential. We are thus particularly taken with the strategy of CEMEX, a cement company based in Mexico, for the way it has adroitly exploited a new unit of business and key metrics to create marketbusting opportunities in the cement business. From its roots as a regional player in Mexico only, the company has aggressively driven growth worldwide, with the result that CEMEX is among the top global players in its industry.

When Lorenzo Zambrano joined what was then a regional Mexican cement company in 1968, the firm's core business involved highly commoditized cement manufacturing plants. When he became CEO in 1985, he inherited a major headache: a chaotic readymix concrete business. The problem with ready-mix concrete is that it is perishable; it begins to set almost as soon as it is loaded into the truck. Couple perishability with unpredictable demand, and you have a mess. Uncertainties about the labor supply, traffic, weather, and financing tended to make customers' need projections unrealistic. So CEMEX could be caught trying to deliver concrete to customers who weren't ready to use it, while other customers were often caught without concrete when they needed it. Even when customers could anticipate their needs, constant changes made keeping track of contracts and changes to contracts an administrative headache.

The conventional unit of business in the concrete industry is cubic yards of concrete. But this unit of business didn't reflect the problems either with perishability or with unpredictable customer demand—two factors that really drove performance for CEMEX's customers. Moreover, the value of the concrete as a commodity pales in comparison with the value to the customer of having the concrete at the right time—delivery and ancillary services are worth far more as a proportion of the customers' wallet than the concrete itself. This is a situation in which what the company sells is far less important than the activities surrounding it.

Zambrano concluded that he would have to look at the business through a different lens if he was to make strategic headway. He decided to change his focus from the concrete itself to getting paid instead for what customers really valued—having the concrete at the right time. Thus, the focus moved to the extent to which his perishable goods were delivered within a timing window that worked for both his company and his customers—neither delaying his deliveries so long that the ready-mix had to be dumped nor making customers with expensive construction crews lose valuable time waiting for him to deliver.

The question, then, was how to change the way the delivery window was managed. When Zambrano started thinking about this, his company operated six independent concrete-mixing plants, each with an independent fleet of delivery trucks. CEMEX wrestled with unpredictable traffic and problems with raw materials and delivery. Its customers struggled with similar problems in preparing their sites for delivery. The net result was that changes to the agreed-upon delivery schedules were constant, causing losses, stress, and frustration on the part of both customers and supplier.

Zambrano's solution began with changing the unit of business. Rather than look only at the amount of cement delivered, he resolved to sell (and charge for) cement delivered within a desired delivery window. The original proposal to customers was that after they contracted with CEMEX, they needed to provide only three hours' notice to arrange delivery. CEMEX guaranteed their supply. In return, customers would pay a bit more for that guarantee than they would pay for cubic yards delivered. More recently, technology initiatives have helped CEMEX to further slash its delivery window from three hours to twenty minutes, making deliveries within that window 98 percent of the time.[7]

For CEMEX to pull this off, it had to develop entirely new capabilities measured by a new set of key metrics. For insight, the company studied other firms that faced the dilemma of matching supply to unpredictable demand, including emergency call centers, ambulance systems, and parcel carriers such as Federal Express. The CEMEX executives learned several things. First, to succeed in an unpredictable demand situation, they needed systems that could adjust the allocation of resources in real time. Second, workflows needed to account for reciprocal interactions among various operating units so that a change in one part of the system was immediately recognized and adjusted to by the others. And finally, a substantial enabler was digital technology.

These insights led to a major company redesign. CEMEX broke apart its plant-centered model. In the new strategy, production was viewed on a regional basis, with links between plants and trucks created on a digital platform. Mobile communications networks linked plants within a region and coordinated the deliveries by all trucks and the production of ready-mix by all plants. In this way, multiple trucks could be serviced by multiple mixing plants to serve any site, coordinated by a central regional scheduling and communications center. Instead of disruptive change orders, the system allowed CEMEX to adjust, in real time, which trucks were bound where. Customers who unexpectedly needed cement could be served, often by shipments originally destined for customers who had requested delayed delivery. Patterns across the entire region could then be analyzed to diminish the extent to which CEMEX was caught by surprise.

After an initial investment in regional communications centers with mobile phone systems connecting the center to plants and to trucks, the system blossomed into a global communications and scheduling capability comprising three components: a global communications system called CEMEXNET, which links every truck and plant via satellite; a tracking, scheduling, and routing system known as Dynamic Synchronization of Operations, which coordinates customer orders with mixing plant and truck availability; and a digital system that links plants, offices, and customers on the Internet.

This new set of capabilities allows CEMEX to deliver same-day service, unlimited order changes by the customer, and a 98 percent reliability of delivery within a twenty-minute window (compared with the original four hours)—with a discount to customers of 5 percent per five-minute delay! Its new capabilities, coupled with astute leadership and financial acumen, has allowed CEMEX to grow from a regional Mexican firm to the third-largest cement and ready-mix concrete supplier in the world. The company delivers nearly $2 billion worth of cement and ready-mix in thirty countries, primarily in emerging economies where the same scheduling challenges prevail as in Mexico.

Detailed Key Metrics Analysis

The first step in developing a set of key metrics is to construct a table of financials that reflects the basic financial performance parameters of your business and, if you have the data, allows you to compare yourself with the top competitors in your industry.[8]

Table 4-1 shows the CEMEX example. The first row specifies the unit of business you are using as well as those used by competitors. In the case of the CEMEX ready-mix business, the unit of business is the number of deliveries of truckloads of ready-mix within the specified time window. Your job here is to look first at whether your competitors are using the same or different units of business and to decide whether the time is right to change the rules of the game by changing the unit of business.

Following the specification of the unit of business, the table is divided into four categories. First are the various direct costs that increase as the unit of business increases. In the case of CEMEX, two such costs are the average total cost of ready-mix raw materials and the average total cost of drivers per load discharged. To get the ratio of net revenues to direct costs, which is a measure of direct cost productivity, you divide the average net revenues per load by each of these costs.

If you have data for the competitors, compare your results with competitors' figures in the remaining columns.[9] This will indicate where you are outperforming or underperforming relative to the competition. Brainstorm with your team how you might significantly improve on the best direct cost ratio in each row along with the new skills, assets, and system improvements it would take to do so. If you do not have competitors' figures, inspect your firm-specific column for the smallest ratios. Think through what prevents you from improving the ratio.

Next, look at the various fixed costs your firm is incurring as you conduct business. For CEMEX, three significant fixed costs are trucking operations overhead, mixing plant overhead, and sales and administration overhead. If you divide these into the gross operating

TABLE 4-1

CEMEX Key Metric Analysis

	Your Firm's Metric (in this case, CEMEX)	Competitor A	Competitor B	Competitor C, etc.
Unit of business	Truck delivery on site within desired delivery window			
Direct cost productivity ratios				
Profit/dollar of unit costs 1	Net revenues/Direct materials cost per load			
Profit/dollar of unit costs 2	Net revenues/Direct driver cost per load			
Etc.				
Fixed cost productivity ratios				
Profit/major fixed cost 1	Gross operating profits/ Total trucking operation overhead			
Profit/major fixed cost 2	Gross operating profits/ Total mixing plant overhead			
Etc.				
Asset productivity ratios				
Profit/dollar asset type 1	Net profits/Total truck assets			
Profit/dollar asset type 2	Net profits/Total mixing plant assets			
Etc.				
Revenue productivity ratios				
Profit/dollar of revenue type 1	Net profits/Ready-mix revenues			
Profit/dollar of revenue type 2	N/A			
Etc.				

profits of your firm, you will get an indication of your fixed cost productivity; low numbers mean that you are incurring a lot of fixed costs to earn your operating profits. As before, look first across the rows to see where you are under- or outperforming competitors, and brainstorm ideas to radically increase your fixed cost productivity. Assess the new skills, assets, and systems it would take to do it.

Next, do the same thing for asset productivity and for revenue productivity—the measure of the amount of revenue it takes to generate a dollar of profits.

Fitch Ratings recently credited CEMEX with doing an excellent job of improving its business and financial profile since 1999. Among the strengths noted by the Fitch analyst are CEMEX's excellent generation of free cash flow, which grew in the period 1999–2001 from $860 million to $1.1 billion. Free cash flow generation is a direct outcome of CEMEX's highly productive operating model.

Its productivity has allowed CEMEX to rapidly pay down the debt it took on to make acquisitions. Fitch also observes CEMEX's "solid track record for meeting its financial targets" and its "production cost advantage vis-à-vis most competitors due to its ability to share best-management and operational practices and transfer production technology among its businesses."[10] The advantages generated by CEMEX's improved key ratios have had significant positive effects on its investment attractiveness.

MarketBuster Prospecting

To begin prospecting for potential marketbusters, it's useful to have your leadership team brainstorm potential alternatives to your current unit of business. If you sell a product, ask yourself whether it might be bundled with a service. If you sell a component, perhaps you could sell a complete solution. If you sell a service, perhaps some customers might like it delivered as a turn-key activity or priced as a package of modules.

With a list of potential new units of business in hand, see whether you have an opportunity to change your business along the lines of eight patterns we identified among firms that dramatically improved their competitive position by changing what they sold, or dramatically improved the way they did business with an existing unit of business. As before, we'll continue with the move numbers from the previous chapter. The eight strategic moves are as follows:

Move #13: Radically change the unit of business

Move #14: Radically improve your productivity

Move #15: Improve your cash flow velocity

Move #16: Change the way you use assets

Move #17: Improve your customers' key metrics

Move #18: Improve your customers' personal productivity

Move #19: Help improve your customers' cash flow

Move #20: Help improve your customers' quality

Move #13: Radically Change the Unit of Business

The first place to prospect for marketbusting moves is to look for an opportunity to rethink the way your industry does business.

Example: Changing the Unit of Business in Television from Sales of Advertising to Sales of User Subscriptions. Often, new technologies or changes in regulations can provide the impetus to rethink the way an industry does business. Consider the evolution of television broadcasting. For many years, TV broadcasting operated on a model in which consumers received free television content that was paid for by advertising shown during the programs (or they paid a flat licensing fee to receive limited programming, as in the United Kingdom). For broadcasters, business was driven largely by the ability of programs to attract mass audiences having desirable demographics, which could then be exploited in advertising sales.

Not long ago, however, innovators such as Ted Turner of Turner Broadcasting System in the United States and Rupert Murdoch of News Corp. came up with a then-heretical idea: What about offering a television service that people would actually pay for on a subscription basis? Skeptics believed that there was no future in such a concept. After all, who would willingly pay for something they could receive for free?

In fits and starts, the satellite and cable-based pay television systems have proven that given the right incentives—such as better reception, more choices of content, access to targeted programming, and the absence of infuriating commercials—people are prepared to pay for television. This dramatically shifted the unit of business from a reliance purely on advertisers to a new model, in which cable and satellite subscriptions provided a solid revenue base that operators could use to build infrastructure and offer new kinds of products. This in turn has created some of the infrastructure on which cable-based Internet-access businesses rely. The point is that altering the basic economic structure of the industry by rethinking the unit of business has led to dramatic new opportunities. As we mentioned earlier, such changes are also evident in the radio business and in other advertising-dependent industries.

Example: Changing the Unit of Business from Promotional Printed Matter to Promotional Services and Solutions. Changes in technology, along with commoditization and aggressive sourcing consolidation by customers, have caused severe price pressure on printers and indeed have sparked many exits from the business. Privately held Madden Communications, however, has escaped the commodity trap by shifting its business definition from providing printing to providing the communications that the printing is designed to create.

In 1988, Madden operated pretty much as a conventional printing house, with a unit of business of individual print jobs. After winning a contract to print one hundred thousand in-store display ads for one of America's largest food companies, company salesman Jim Donahugh visited a target supermarket to see his product on display. Much to his dismay, the displays were nowhere to be seen, nor were they visible at several other stores he then checked. Donahugh found that this was not unusual at all. Operating on very thin margins and with thousands of stockkeeping units to manage, supermarket owners often didn't (or couldn't) take the time to display promotions properly. Donahugh also found out that Madden's own customers, the packaged goods companies, often overordered promotional materials as insurance against running short. In both cases, the end result was either a failure to communicate with their potential customers or money wasted on printed matter that wasn't used.

From these insights, Madden developed a direct-to-store printing and shipping program. Instead of buying individual printing jobs, its customers now contract for a long-term promotional arrangement in which Madden prints only the required number of displays and promotional materials and then manages their distribution and installation on-site. Together with its changed unit of business, Madden changed the customers it sought to serve—moving from many smaller customers to a few large ones with whom it could build long-term relationships. The larger customers appreciated and were willing to pay for Madden's capabilities. Madden naturally had to change the way it did business. From a relatively low-level, standard type of selling, it has now migrated to a partnership position with its customers, in which Madden people try to really understand the customers' businesses and objectives.

Madden's revenues grew from $5 million in 1980 to $10 million in 1990 to $120 million in 1997, in an industry many had come to regard as hopelessly mature. Year 2000 sales were $132,429,000. In 2002 Madden generated more than half a million dollars in revenue for each of its two hundred fifty employees.

Prospecting Questions for Changing the Unit of Business

Probe the following questions. Keep at it until you are convinced that you have really gotten people to think.

Can you generate revenues via a different unit of business?

Can you charge for what you offer in a different way?

Can you incur costs and make payments in a different way?

Can you shift the emphasis in how you charge customers from what you traditionally provide to what they might value (for instance, going from a part of a solution to the actual solution)?

Can you create better incentives for your people by changing the unit of business (for instance, going from an incentive system based on business unit performance to one based on the total relationship between your company and your customer)?

Would some other way of charging for what you sell be more convenient, less effortful, or easier to explain to your customers?

Move #14: Radically Improve Your Productivity

Some firms established and sustained strong positions because they achieved consistently superior productivity. With this market-busting move, your aim is to identify ways to dramatically enhance your key productivity ratios in a way that rivals will find difficult to imitate. Note that here, unlike the previous move of changing your unit of business, you are essentially using the same measurements as others, but achieving better performance. When you can do this in a credible and measurable way, investors notice! These moves have the advantage that they are relatively easy to communicate to the investing community.

Example: Using E-commerce and Supply Chain Solutions to Eliminate Inefficiencies and Boost Productivity.
Lamons Gasket Company (http://www.lamonsgasket.com) is the largest manufacturer and distributor of static sealing solutions for the petrochemical, refining, nuclear, OEM, pulp, and paper industries. The company, an $80 million subsidiary of MetalDyne Corporation, manufactures and distributes more than one hundred thousand standard and special-order products, ranging from gaskets to an extensive line of packings, threaded barstock, nuts, bolts, and screws.

Until recently, customer orders were manually entered into the enterprise resource planning (ERP) system. Ken Frigo, Lamons's executive vice president, observed that "Customers would either phone in or fax an order, using their own language to describe what they needed. One of our thirty customer service representatives would then have to translate this order into the correct Lamons format and part numbers . . . Because an average order is less than $500, this thirty to sixty minutes of manual work to get each order into our systems presented significant costs."[11] Indeed, relative to the value of the sale, this level of inefficiency was devastating to profits. It was also costly to customers. Let's not forget that someone on the customer side is spending the same thirty to sixty minutes!

Lamons decided to tackle the problem by building an integrated e-commerce Web site. The site enabled customers to find and order goods. The solution allows for customer-specific pricing, lets customers pay for orders with either a credit card or a traditional purchase order, and permits multiple ship-to and bill-to options. In addition to automating the product-selection and order-entry process, having a Web site that was connected to its ERP system enabled Lamons to provide customers with the information they need without having to contact a Lamons customer service representative, something that has led to further reductions in the company's customer service costs. Lamons achieved an advantage by implementing this solution quickly.[12]

Prospecting Questions for Radically Improving Productivity

Can you dramatically enhance your productivity by deploying new technology?

- Direct cost productivity
- Fixed cost productivity
- Asset productivity
- Revenue productivity

Can you leapfrog your competition in productivity? Look especially for situations where their resources are already committed to something else (such as integrating a large merger).

Can you eliminate time-wasting repetitive activities to enhance productivity? Can you figure out how to eliminate transaction costs (such as internal reviews and approvals) by automating some of your internal control practices, thus boosting productivity?

A cautionary note is in order, however. Given Lamons's success, its competitors are sure to emulate this approach to supply and ordering. When they do, the e-commerce solution will no longer differentiate Lamons but instead will become a competitive prerequisite. Then the challenge for the company will be to identify the next major productivity advance if it continues to offer the same things to its customers.

Move #15: Improve Your Cash Flow Velocity

Another move that can give you better profitability is to speed up the cash velocity of your business. Even if you don't change anything about your business model, speeding everything up can create surprising positive outcomes, because profits can pour in more rapidly. The idea is that the higher your cash flow velocity, the less working capital you need, and the more effectively your assets are used. This will show up as an improvement in key ratios relative to competition.

Example: A Coordinated Attack on Time Lags in the Mortgage Business. American Home Mortgage Holdings (AHMH) has accelerated its cash velocity by building systems that let it take advantage of a boom in home mortgage refinancing. With interest rates at historic lows, there has been a dramatic increase in the availability of debt capital. (For example, the Federal Reserve reports that as of February 2004, a ten-year treasury bond carried an interest rate of around 4 percent.[13]) Coupled with cheaper money, real estate values increased significantly throughout the 1990s. This combination of contextual factors has made it attractive for many homeowners to use their home equity, often by borrowing against it or by refinancing their mortgages at lower rates. As of this writing, most borrowers can replace their existing financing and harvest 10 to 20 percent over their existing debt with very little change in debt-service coverage.

Historically, AHMH focused on home buyers rather than on refinancing, but it was quick to recognize the opportunities in refinancing and move aggressively to capitalize on them. Aside from representing a large market, refinancers are also attractive because they can be persuaded to refinance, unlike home buyers for whom the activity is linked in time to the purchase of a home. AHMH has identified ways to speed capturing and placing loans throughout the mortgage system. It places deals with large refinancers such as Fannie Mae and the government-owned Freddie Mac, thus enabling profits on the spread between the interest rate charged to consumers and the interest rate it pays to refinancers. Because its systems interact with large refinancers' systems, it can guarantee credit compliance, place deals, and move the cash quickly. The more deals it can close in the shortest time, the higher its cash flow velocity.

American Home Mortgage also enhances velocity by the use of both highly automated systems and highly focused bricks-and-mortar infrastructure. It originates and sells mortgage loans through its MortgageSelect.com Web site, which provides customers with twenty-four-hour access to interest rates and product terms. At this site customers can also lock in interest rates, file preapproval applications, check the status of pending applications, and obtain credit reports. In addition, the Web site contains calculation tools that determine the affordability of financing, letting potential customers prescreen their qualification for various loan levels. AHMH complements its virtual interface with seventy field offices in several states (although it does a much higher volume of business through electronic mechanisms than it does face to face).

AHMH is forecast to grow at 28 percent per year, a rate that, according to analysts, puts this company in the excellent or outperform category. The company is expected to continue to produce operational results that are well above average, with relatively consistent returns over the long term.

Example: Getting Paid for Accelerating Bad Debt Collection. National Credit Systems (NCS), founded in 1984, has based its entire competitive strategy on the acceleration of cash flows. NCS is an accounts receivable management firm, a polite term for collection agency.

Unlike most collection agencies, NCS does not charge its customers a percentage of the money it can collect for them. Instead, it charges a fee per account of $20. This translates into large client savings relative to its competition, because the average collection agency retains 40 percent of collections as fees, whereas NCS retains a mere 8 percent. Furthermore, any money recovered is sent directly to the client, and therefore NCS does not delay client cash flow.

How can NCS possibly make money by keeping less of what it collects and giving most of its cash flow directly back to customers? The answer lies in the recovery ratio, a key ratio that drives profitability in the world of collections. NCS achieves an unusually high

Prospecting Questions for Improving Cash Flow Velocity

How might you accelerate the cash flow velocity of your firm?

Could you eliminate or reduce inventory?

Might you delay payments to others?

Can you speed up receipts from your customers?

Can you generate cash before you have to incur costs (such as with Dell's "build to order" computers)?

Can you speed up the ordering cycle of your customers?

Can you get paid more frequently over the lifetime of a contract?

Can you automate the payment stream so that manual delays don't hold up incoming cash?

Can you make sure that your invoicing mechanisms are easy for your customers to respond to, so that you don't create additional payment delays?

Have you checked to see whether you might link up with customers electronically to speed payments?

Have you explored technologies such as direct-deposit or lock-boxes to speed payments?

recovery rate of 57 percent compared with the national average of 18 percent. The company has built a powerful set of collections capabilities by rethinking standard practice in its industry. The industry took it for granted that collection effectiveness increased with the cost and complexity of the three major methods of collection. At the low cost and complexity end was sending letters. Next was telephone calling, and finally (the most expensive) was taking legal action. NCS revisited this set of assumptions and came to a surprising conclusion: The least expensive method (letters) was ultimately the most effective—some 80 percent of all bad debt collected in fact came from a transaction initiated by a letter—but incumbent players were not using it very effectively.

NCS succeeded in increasing collection volume, based on the old technology. With high volumes, NCS could charge clients less than the industry standard, further increasing volumes as clients appreciated the better prices. Not only did NCS accelerate its own cash flows, but it also improved the bottom line of its customers by improving their cash flow.

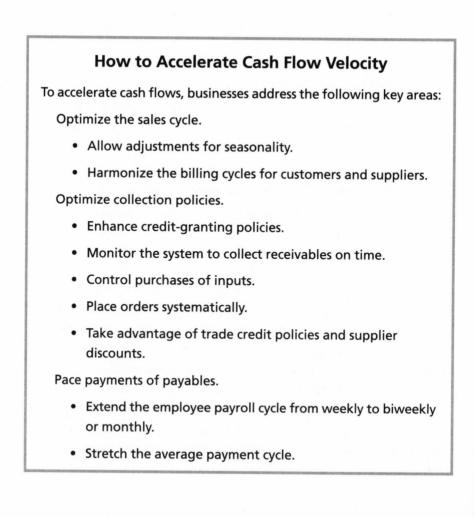

How to Accelerate Cash Flow Velocity

To accelerate cash flows, businesses address the following key areas:

Optimize the sales cycle.

- Allow adjustments for seasonality.
- Harmonize the billing cycles for customers and suppliers.

Optimize collection policies.

- Enhance credit-granting policies.
- Monitor the system to collect receivables on time.
- Control purchases of inputs.
- Place orders systematically.
- Take advantage of trade credit policies and supplier discounts.

Pace payments of payables.

- Extend the employee payroll cycle from weekly to biweekly or monthly.
- Stretch the average payment cycle.

Leverage bank credit policies.

- Monitor how fast sales receipts are credited to bank accounts.
- Establish a line of credit for negative cash flow periods.
- Ensure that loan repayment terms remain "in sync" with the cash flow cycle.

Manage assets efficiently.

- Carry inventory on consignment.
- Assess leasing versus buying assets.

Plan tax strategy.

- Maximize tax reductions and deferrals.

Balance cash flow and profitability objectives.

- Increase sales without increasing collections.
- Rapidly pass on increased costs from suppliers to customers.
- Automatically adjust prices as costs of inputs vary.

Move #16: Change the Way You Use Assets

A powerful area to probe is whether you can do anything differently from others in your industry to reduce asset intensity or to better use those assets that you must have. In most industries, a key metric used to assess performance is return on assets, a direct assessment of how effectively you are using your assets to drive profits.

Example: Using Scale to Reduce Asset Intensity for Both You and Your Customers. Quanta Computers was founded in May 1988 by Chinese entrepreneur Barry Lam to address the challenge of asset intensity facing many notebook computer manufacturers. Lam combined the promise of reducing customers' assets with the ability to spread Quanta's asset base across companies worldwide. This strategy successfully fueled the dramatic growth of Quanta as a reliable sales and manufacturing partner to notebook PC vendors such as Apple, Dell, Gateway, and Fujitsu-Siemens.

Quanta has two major asset productivity drivers. First, it serves many customers as a contract manufacturer and design partner, a practice that has the effect of using manufacturing capacity more effectively than any one company could do in-house. Second, Quanta helps its customers reduce their asset intensity by using Quanta to manufacture some or preferably all the components they need. In this way, Quanta has effectively played a two-way game of reducing asset intensity. Sales in 2002 exceeded $4 billion.

Prospecting Questions for Changing the Way You Use Assets

Can you reduce the asset intensity of your business by outsourcing some activities to specialist providers?

Can you eliminate the need to own certain assets?

Can you utilize assets owned by someone else on an as-needed basis?

Can you use assets more effectively—for instance, by extending the time of day in which they are used or by using remote electronics to operate them?

Might you be able to pool your assets with those of other firms and reduce the asset intensity for the whole group?

Can you change fixed assets to variable assets—for instance, by establishing utilization contracts with suppliers for certain services?

Can you help your customers reduce their fixed asset burden by taking on their assets and charging them for usage?

Move #17: Improve Your Customers' Key Metrics

Another powerful application of key metrics analysis is to focus the analysis on helping your customers. Helping your customers improve their performance generates a stronger, more robust, more profitable, more loyal base of clients that are both more willing and more able to buy from you. To the extent that your system is critical to or embedded in the way they do business, you can also achieve a certain amount of competitive sustainability.

How can you figure out how to help your customers? You could start by asking them—they usually can be quite articulate about the pain points in their businesses. Next, you could look at their financial statements and (if appropriate) assessments of them from knowledgeable outside sources, such as stock analysts (see the box earlier in this chapter, Hunting Down High-Potential Key Metrics). When you know what your customers get graded on, consider how you might help them improve their grades.

Can you help your customers improve productivity? Increasingly, this means providing them with tools they can use to take best advantage of the skills, assets, and systems they have in place.

Example: Swiss Re Uses Administrative Reinsurance to Free Up Capital for Insurance Company Clients. A persistent problem for insurance companies is what are termed "closed blocks" of in-force life and health insurance. Because an insurance policy can be in force for a long time, the issuing company can find itself lumbered with decades of obligations that tie up capital which could be put to more strategic uses. Moreover, old books of business are often supported by legacy IT systems, which can easily become an expensive nightmare to maintain and run, also costing the companies money for staff and computer systems they would love to be able to eliminate.

Swiss Re (Swiss Reinsurance Company) has developed a solution for this problem that creates dramatic positive effects for its clients. Through its Admin Re line of business, Swiss Re takes on closed blocks of in-force life and health insurance either by acquiring them outright or by reinsuring them. It then administers the policies using its own proprietary business processes, often partnering with professional administrators to maximize the efficiencies gained. The advantage for customers is that they can eliminate the need to tie up capital to support this business, reduce the personnel costs linked to historical business (which are thus not available to develop new business), and eliminate legacy systems. This shows up for customers as an improvement in their combined ratio (as explained earlier), a key metric used to assess insurance industry performance. In the seven years (as of this writing) that Swiss Re has offered the Admin Re solution, it has grown the numbers of policies managed to over four and a half million, making this service one of the Swiss company's fastest-growing lines of business.

Prospecting Questions for Improving Customers' Key Metrics

Have your marketbusting team gather the following information:

What are the key numbers your customers seek to achieve? (Be explicit.)

How do your customers measure this outcome?

What are the key ratios in your customers' businesses?

What are some ways to

- Help your customers improve their key ratios (financial, operating, investment)? Conceive of a better way to help customers hit the numbers they care about (market share, cash flow, EBITDA, revenue growth, profit)?[14]
- Help customers better understand what really drives success in their businesses?

Can you find ways to improve your customers' productivity?

Can you help customers make better use of their assets? Their working capital?

Can you take over some aspect of your customers' operations that they find burdensome?

Move #18: Improve Your Customers' Personal Productivity

What asset productivity is to a commercial customer, time saving and convenience are to a consumer. Whenever you can see a way to make something that is irritatingly complex more convenient and quick to accomplish, you may have the seeds of a marketbuster with high potential. Most people can readily recite how well-intentioned companies do things that drive them crazy, usually because they lead them to waste time or induce delays in meeting their objectives. For instance, banks and insurance companies force you to obtain information from third parties before they will do business with you; service desks run you through the "press 1, press 2" voice-mail gauntlet; retail establishments subject you to the same checkout delays whether you are buying a truckload or a single item; companies require that you remember the numbers (order numbers, service tag numbers, customer numbers) that they gave you in the first place; and on and on. Solve the irritations and customers will often gratefully reciprocate by increasing your sales volumes or paying you more.

Example: Simplifying the Process of Obtaining Financial Services by Having Providers Compete for Your Business. Just as AHMH figured out how to accelerate the process of refinancing, mortgage broker LendingTree built its business on making the process less onerous from a consumer point of view. It uses Web-based technology to dramatically reduce customer acquisition costs and obtain leads on loans. In contrast to the AHMH model, in which the company itself is a broker of mortgages, LendingTree acts to link networks of mortgage providers to give consumers maximum choice and improve the competitiveness of the offers they consider. They send requests to their network of lenders, who return bids. Consumers can also use the service to choose from a list of mortgages, credit cards, and home equity, auto, and personal loans. Unlike a conventional bank, LendingTree's model claims to empower borrowers by making lenders apply to them, rather than making borrowers apply to the lender.

Prospecting Questions for
Improving Your Customers' Personal Productivity

Can you change the way you do business to save your customers time?

Can you reduce the number of steps a customer must take to do business with you?

Can you eliminate hassles and annoyances from your transactions (for instance, forcing the customer to repeat information on forms, to collect information from different places, or to get material from third parties before they can do business with you).

Can you create a single point of interface between your company and your customers?

Can you address some customer issues with a single interaction rather than with multiple interactions?

Can you routinize customer-facing activities to make them faster?

Can you find ways to improve the personal productivity of your customers' staff? On the job? In their private lives?

Participating lenders pay a transaction fee upon submitting the loan application and again when the loan is closed. Consumers who use LendingTree do not pay a service fee. From 1998 through 2001, LendingTree processed more than 5 million credit requests and generated $10 billion in transaction volume. In 2003, LendingTree was acquired by InterActive Corp., inspired no doubt by a 74 percent sales increase from 2001 to 2002.

Move #19: Help Improve Your Customers' Cash Flow

Just as you will look better in the analysts' eyes by improving your cash flow metrics (see move #15), your customers will look better to their analysts to the extent that they can do the same. Many of the same techniques we described above are applicable here, but instead of trying to get better within your own operations, you are going to try to sell something to customers that helps them improve their cash flows. Alternatively, you might differentiate your company by being the one that allows customers to operate more effectively when they work with you—for instance, by requiring that they stock less inventory or by moving faster on orders received.

Example: Helping Companies Make Better Asset Utilization Decisions. The rapid growth of software company SAS Institute is attributable largely to the accelerating effect it has on customers' ability to make better decisions faster, thus using their assets more productively. SAS provides integrated enterprise information-delivery and e-business solutions. Among SAS's remarkable qualities are that it benefits from the lowest employee turnover in its industry and enjoys a 98 percent renewal rate among customers, many of whom could not conceive of doing without its software.

By becoming a true strategic partner in which its developments are driven largely by customer demand for improved operations, SAS has enjoyed a long track record of solid profits. The Institute has a balance sheet free of debt and a projected annual growth rate of more than 20 percent. In 2002 its sales topped $1 billion.

Similar rapid growth has been enjoyed in the whole enterprise resource management area, with firms such as SAP building on clients' hunger to better utilize their resources to achieve market-busting outcomes.

Example: Leveraging the Most Time-Intensive Part of the PC Repair Process with Logistics Expertise. Package delivery firm United Parcel Service (UPS) has begun to branch out from its core business of package delivery into an array of businesses, all of which are designed to help customers' cash flow. Under the rubric "synchronizing commerce," UPS performs a variety of services that go well beyond the traditional pickup and

---

Prospecting Questions for Improving Customers' Cash Flow

Refer to the questions in #15 with respect to your cash flow velocity. Ask also:

Can you change the way you do business to help customers get revenues in more quickly or delay expenditures?

Can you help customers better coordinate their activities to eliminate cash flow losses due to internal inefficiencies?

Can you change the way you do business to make some fixed costs variable for your customers?

Can you eliminate "nuisance" payments for your customers?

---

delivery. One recent move, for instance, has UPS employees doing the repair work for Toshiba laptops. As Mark Simons, a general manager of Toshiba's digital products division was reported as saying, "Moving a unit around and getting replacement parts consumes most of the time. . . . The actual service only takes about an hour."[15] By taking over both the shipping of warrantee repairs and the repair, UPS eliminates steps in the process, removes the need for PC makers to employ a maintenance staff, integrates the repair and shipping activity, and, most importantly, reduces the time that a broken PC is not in the hands of its owner. Just as the management of CEMEX realized that the time window for cement delivery had value beyond the cement itself, the management of UPS is capitalizing on the fact that the timing of item delivery can have value well beyond the items alone.

Move #20: Help Improve Your Customers' Quality

Another opportunity for marketbusting concerns improving the quality of your customers' offerings. If you can do something for customers that lets them credibly claim superior quality or that allows them to provide state-of-the-art quality at a competitive price, you have the potential to gain enormous loyalty, along with all the benefits of becoming embedded as a central element in your customers' business model. The reason quality is so powerful as a key metric is that it influences many other metrics—for manufactured products, for instance, repairs and returns can have an impact on working capital, employee costs, customer loyalty, and return on assets. Even small improvements in quality that eliminate warrantee repairs can have a substantial follow-on impact.

Example: KLA-Tencor Helps Eliminate Defects in Computer Chips. In the semiconductor business, a hugely important key metric is "yield"—meaning the number of defect-free chips that come out of the manufacturing process. Let yields go down, the profitability of the whole enterprise is hurt. Improve yields, and a company can make more chips for less investment in assets (which is considerable in the semiconductor business; plants can cost upwards of $3 billion each). KLA-Tencor makes equipment and software that can detect defects in silicon wafers. By using the KLA-Tencor process, manufacturers can improve yields throughout their system.

Example: Six Sigma Everything! An entire industry has grown up around a concept pioneered by Motorola, that of dramatically reducing the defects in manufactured products through the rigorous application of statistical process control techniques. The concept has become central to the strategies of many manufacturing organizations, premised on the simple idea that if quality is designed into a process, dramatic improvements in asset utilization and other key metrics will follow.

Prospecting Questions for Improving Customer Quality

Can you redesign the way you do business with customers to help them improve quality metrics?

Can you offer examples or advice to customers to help them improve quality?

Can you offer consulting solutions to improve customer quality (or related concepts such as safety)?

Can you lead your industry in creating more high-quality offerings than it does today?

Can you provide quality-oriented feedback to your customers so that they can respond in real time?

Action Steps for Redefining Key Metrics

Step 1: Identify your own unit of business and associated key metrics.

Step 2: Identify the obstacles that prevent you from achieving higher performance on these key metrics.

Step 3: Assess how you do relative to your competition. Do they use the same metrics? How do you stack up?

Step 4: Determine which customer segments you serve. What are the key metrics that matter to them? How well do you do in helping them achieve desirable results? Could you improve your value to them by offering a different unit of business (for example, by switching from selling a product to selling a more comprehensive solution)?

Step 5: Assess what new capabilities you would need if you were to change units of business. How would you measure success? What are your key assumptions with respect to customer adoption? How will you sell this idea to customers?

Step 6: Decide on a marketing plan. How can you communicate the advantages of this new unit to your customers? To your stock analysts?

Step 7: Carefully examine the implementation challenge. Refer to the DRAT table in chapter 7, and try to identify obvious pitfalls as you roll out this shift in strategy.

5

Exploit Industry Shifts

So far, you have looked for opportunities that lie in better understanding customers, in reconfiguring your offerings to various customer segments, and in changing the key ratios that dictate the profitability of a strategy. In this chapter, you'll learn how firms have taken advantage of opportunities to capitalize on changes that affect all the competitors in their industries. The perspective here builds on a traditional preoccupation with industry-level phenomena, but instead of looking at them as relatively stable, we see them as dynamic. The idea is that when a major industry shift is in the works, the thundering herd will tend to move in the same direction. You can create significant advantages by playing the game differently.

In this chapter you will find many examples of companies that have done just that. The process is to first determine the potential for major industry-level change and then figure out whether you can do one of three things: (1) exploit your insights into a pending change through the action of an external force, (2) take advantage of second-order effects brought about by the change, or (3) introduce a disruptive change and benefit from it.

Consider a capital-intensive industry in which capacity utilization is a major driver for profitability. Competitive behavior in such industries is predictable. When demand exceeds supply, all players make a fortune, and that encourages them to expand capacity. As the new capacity comes onstream, demand is satiated, and everyone drops prices to try to maintain profitable volumes. Profitability across the industry sinks.[1] Recognizing this pattern, astute players might capitalize on it by devising a way to eliminate the structural causes of cycles; exploit it by creating the capability to create capacity at the peak without being forced to preserve it during the low period; or benefit by becoming a second-order capacity broker.

A prepared firm might make a lot of money by, for example, locking up or securing capacity in times of shortage, or by incorporating the kind of flexibility that lets it respond quickly to short-term demand pressures in whichever markets they appear.[2] Another approach is to provide products or services that help your customers cope with cycles in their industries. Examples include building modular factories, converting plants to use multiple fuels, and linking disparate producers to increase or decrease supply.[3]

This chapter describes ideas for marketbusters that can help you capitalize on insights into your industry that have so far escaped your competition.

Industry Dynamics

In the early days of any industry, firms experiment. Technologies, units of business, features, sales channels, marketing pitches, branding, and so on are up for grabs.[4] Over time, players learn which approaches work better than others, and the variety in the industry begins to decline. Dozens or hundreds of new entrants also decrease to a few that have come up with a workable formula for competing in the new space. Eventually, certain practices, technologies, and ideas come to be regarded as legitimate and central to the industry. At this stage, these elements become taken for granted, and business as usual commences.[5]

Interestingly, when an industry starts to change, it often seems as though every strategist is reading the same recipe book, and soon firms are rolling out a horde of similar strategies. Typically the initial reaction to industrywide change is denial that there is a problem. This is followed shortly by resistance to the problem and attempts to reinforce the existing business model.[6] If the change really is fundamental, the resistance period is typically followed either by begrudging acceptance on the part of the incumbents or a shift in players within the industry as those who are no longer competitive in the new space leave and others enter.

Thus, as of this writing the recording studios are all trying to put roadblocks in the way of digital music and video distribution. The pattern is familiar. When threatened with the incursion of mini-mill technology into their markets, all the incumbent steel companies retreated to higher-margin markets and attempted to cut costs. Faced with the nearly disastrous circumstances of 2002–2003, major airlines globally used the same cut-and-shrink-to-survive strategies to try to overcome years of overcapacity and inflexible route structures. Threatened by the Internet, globalization, and the presumed convergence in financial services, financial companies the world over have been buying their way into "diversified" financial services, believing that demand for one-stop shopping will offer substantial customer value. And the list goes on. Clearly, it is extremely hard for a firm to break away from the industry pack, and yet, equally clearly, this is where the greatest opportunities are likely to be found.

Thriving in an Industry Change

We found three distinctive strategies that characterize firms that were able not only to survive but to thrive in the presence of an industry shift.

The first strategy involved proactive anticipation and exploitation of the shift and its consequences. Intel, for example, perceived that chip speed was no longer the dominant criterion of choice for all but the most demanding users, meaning that some other requirement would become important. For Intel, it is critical that the other requirement not be price, because its model of high investment, R&D, and manufacturing capacity would put the company at a disadvantage in a price-driven world. With the introduction of the new Centrino laptop chip, Intel has anticipated and accelerated the rise of longer battery life and wireless connectivity, rather than raw speed, as the dominant marketing criteria for laptops. Using its position as industry leader, Intel can initiate this shift and exploit it to the fullest. Of course, even mighty Intel is not immune—challenger AMD has made significant inroads, particularly in those lower-end segments that Intel is more reluctant to serve.

A second pattern we observed occurred when firms took advantage of second-order effects of a change in conditions. An expensive labor agreement that leads incumbents to suffer cost increases might lead to the second-order consequence of competitive players moving resources to areas not affected by the increase—as in greenfield developments. This shift can then create opportunities for service companies that can shorten the time to construct such a plant, for lobbyists who can ease local regulatory constraints, and for engineers and architects who have plans at the ready.

A similar second-order motivation can often be detected in firms that relocate their operations. By moving to a different institutional environment, companies can create advantages if competitors are locked into an existing one, creating a second-order opportunity. Citibank, for example, relocated its credit card operations to South Dakota from New York to escape usury laws that limited the interest it could charge to customers on revolving credit card debt.

A third approach is to disrupt things in a way that favors your capabilities and ideally disadvantages others. Hewlett-Packard is aligning itself to do this in the market for photographic printing. Many HP printers come with slots for the memory chips used in digital cameras and with software that allows users to easily copy, print, and store their images. HP makes its money on the printers, the paper, and the inks. This model is enormously threatening to the industry, which has grown up around film and the production of pictures from film: the small photo print shops, the multinational manufacturers of chemicals and paper, and of course the manufacturers of film-based cameras, such as Kodak. Allied with HP are companies such as Sony (nontraditional camera manufacturers) and traditional camera companies such as Olympus and Canon, which are seeking to move their business models into the digital age. If they succeed, the advent of digital imaging is likely to make huge inroads into what was a stable, successful industry by rendering entire functions obsolete.

The Framework of Industry Shifts

The essential feature of an industry shift is that the power held by various parties shifts. Porter long ago pointed out that an industry can go from being attractive for investment to being unattractive to the extent that its structure changes in a way that favors buyers or suppliers, that encourages substitution, or that limits barriers to entry.[7]

One way this occurs is through industry cycles, as mentioned earlier. Another is when a constraint that has kept power relations in balance shifts—as when regulations, technology, or industry standards change. Another type of change occurs through the natural process of industry evolution; as a new industry goes from a startup situation to a more mature one, predictable shifts in power take place. And of course innovations, by changing the cost or logistical routines that have become standard, always have the potential to reconfigure the way current value chains are constructed.

Where to start? Begin by assessing the likelihood of a major change in your industry. Table 5-1 provides some indicative questions you might use.

By combining these four patterns with the three approaches to taking advantage of industry change, we have developed a simple framework, shown in table 5-2, that you can use to structure your thinking about possible industrywide shifts. The result is twelve

TABLE 5-1

Industry Shifts Framework

Pattern of Industry Change	Is it happening? The more yes answers, the more likely the pattern is to be emerging.
Industry swings through cycles of surplus and scarcity	Does capacity increase in steps rather than smooth increments? Are sunk costs for installed capacity substantial? Are there strong incentives for high levels of capacity utilization? Do prices and profits rise sharply when demand exceeds supply? Do large players have an advantage relative to smaller players?
Shift in an industry constraint or barrier	One competitor has introduced an innovation that radically changes the constraints (cost, quality, timing, other) the industry operates under. Regulatory, legal, or social constraints are increasing or decreasing. A credible substitute offering has become available. Entry barriers are increasing or decreasing. The industry appears to be globalizing production and/or marketing.
Increased pace of industry evolution*	The assets and resources that players use in the industry are changing in value (either becoming more or less valuable). The key relationships and activities in the industry are undergoing dramatic change. The rate of new entry to the industry is changing (either dramatically increasing or falling off). Competition is changing—new players are emerging. Industry growth rate is changing—either declining or growing dramatically.
Shift in patterns of costs or bottlenecks causes value chain reordering	A distribution channel is increasing or decreasing in influence. Industry players are vertically integrating or horizontally deintegrating. New intermediaries are emerging in the value chain. Old intermediaries are disappearing in the value chain. Costs in one or more parts of the value chain are radically increasing (or decreasing). New bottlenecks to productivity are emerging.

*For an insightful discussion of industry evolution, see McGahan, A. M. (2004). *How Industries Evolve*. Boston: Harvard Business School Press.

possible strategic moves. We'll list them here, numbering consecutively with the previous chapter as before:

Move #21: End-run predictable industry swings

Move #22: Capitalize on second-order effects of industry cycles

Move #23: Launch a disruptive response to cycles

Move #24: Exploit shifts in industry constraints or barriers

Move #25: Capitalize on second-order effects of shifts in constraints

Move #26: Use a shift in a key constraint to disrupt the industry

Move #27: Exploit your industry's structure for the next life cycle stage

Move #28: Understand the second-order effects of the next stage

Move #29: Redirect, disrupt or alter the evolutionary trajectory

Move #30: Exploit a shift in the value chain

Move #31: Exploit second-order effects of shifts in the value chain

Move #32: Reduce costs or abolish bottlenecks to disrupt the value chain

If you have concluded that one of these four change patterns is happening in your industry, you should consider where you have opportunities to make an end run around the change, benefit from second-order effects, or disrupt things for the competition by accelerating the change.

TABLE 5-2

MarketBuster Prospecting by Exploiting Industry Dynamics

Pattern of Industry Change	Exploit Insights into the Pattern	Take Advantage of Second-Order Effects	Provoke Disruptive Change in the Pattern
Industry swings through cycles of surplus and scarcity	Move #21: End-run predictable industry swings	Move #22: Capitalize on second-order effects of industry cycles	Move #23: Launch a disruptive response to cycles
Shift in an industry constraint or barrier changes power relations	Move #24: Exploit shifts in industry constraints or barriers	Move #25: Capitalize on second-order effects of shifts in constraints	Move #26: Use a shift in a key constraint to disrupt the industry
Industry evolves	Move #27: Exploit your industry's structure for the next life cycle stage	Move #28: Understand the second-order effects of the next stage	Move #29: Redirect, disrupt, or alter the evolutionary trajectory
Shift in patterns of costs or bottlenecks causes value chain reordering	Move #30: Exploit a shift in the value chain	Move #31: Exploit second-order effects of shifts in the value chain	Move #32: Reduce costs or abolish bottlenecks to disrupt the value chain

Let's walk through each of the four industry change patterns and look at examples that might help trigger your own thinking about industry dynamics. At the end of the discussion we provide a list of provocative questions you can ask to see whether a marketbusting opportunity may be present for you.

MarketBuster Prospecting Within Predictable Industry Cycles

The great advantage of cyclical industries is that they are to some extent predictable. The great danger of such industries, however, is that individually rational behavior can lead to collectively absurd results—one of the reasons that cycles persist.[8] Thus, if everyone invests to increase capacity, excess is likely to create incentives for predatory pricing and increased competition. At the same time, no red-blooded executive wants to defer investment in the next-generation plant or in the next great opportunity and then watch helplessly as competitors that benefit from occasional scarcity walk away with the profits. Real estate, semiconductor manufacturing, and insurance are all industries that are heavily cyclical.

Move #21: End-Run Predictable Industry Swings

One way that firms have end-run the opportunities of cyclical surplus and scarcity is to figure out how to create capacity at the peak and maintain low carrying costs at the trough. This suggests an options-oriented approach to capacity creation. If you can think of a creative way to capture some of the peak demand without being stuck with excess capacity in a downturn, you can create considerable value. The option, in such a case, is to address peak demand—creating the capability, without necessarily the obligation, to maintain that level of production capacity over the long term.[9]

Example: Inefficient Peaking Plants Kick in When Prices Rise. The energy industry provides an example of how some firms took advantage of sharp shifts in available demand and supply and subsequent steep changes in prices. Competitors in this industry invested in so-called peaking plants, which were relatively inexpensive to build although less efficient than the state-of-the-art facilities that would be in normal use. Peaking plants are brought online only when prices spike sharply upward, giving the owning firms the capability, but not the obligation, to generate energy from them as the economics of the situation demand. In an industry in which unit prices can shoot up to several thousand times their normal levels, such a response to capacity constraints can create considerable benefits. Together with the peaking plants, many energy companies (including the now-discredited Enron) engaged in sophisticated forms of options-style contracting, giving them the capability to trade units of energy under various combinations of future circumstances.

Example: Partner with Others to Gain Capacity. Other firms have found ways to end-run cycles by combining production resources. Members of cluster manufacturing circles in Italy have been known to compete aggressively for contracts but to cooperate simultaneously in delivering on those contracts. This behavior is premised on the idea that all players benefit when the incentives to create systemic excess capacity are muted. The key principle here is to capture the capability, but not the obligation, to gain capacity if and only if it is needed.[10]

Example: Betting the Company in Semiconductors. As of this writing, a huge marketbuster gamble is playing out in the semiconductor industry. Globally, several huge players are investing to build the next-generation semiconductor fabricating facilities, involving huge sunk investments (on the order of $3 billion per plant).[11] Others, having decided that the fixed investment and cyclical nature of semiconductors create a game they don't wish to play, are betting instead that they will be able to acquire capacity if they need it from contract producers. The gamble concerns which side will retain more power. Those with the fabricating plants run the risk of excess capacity and pressure on prices, and the others run the risk of a lack of capacity, high prices, and the possibility of being shut out or rationed in meeting their needs. Should those building the plants prove right, they stand to make substantial profits on their bet.

Move #22: Capitalize on Second-Order Effects of Industry Cycles

Among the more interesting consequences of cyclical industries is that as an industry moves from cycle to cycle, second-order bottlenecks often emerge. Without competing directly within a cyclical industry, some clever firms have benefited from the second-order consequences cycles create.

Example: Capitalizing on Internet-Driven Demand for Packaging. New Jersey–based Sealed Air Corporation manufactures a wide range of food and protective packaging materials and systems that reach some 80 percent of the world's population. Sealed Air has taken great advantage of a second-order scarcity created by the emergence of Internet-based retailing. Unlike conventional retailing, Internet-based retailing includes the crucial value chain element of packaging goods for shipment. If the packaging doesn't work, the rest of the offering doesn't work.

Sealed Air has used two main strategies to capitalize on the new primacy of packaging for entire industry segments. The first approach focuses on providing a full packaging solution, which includes the launch of www.e-packaging.com. This interactive Web site walks business customers through their entire shipping and packaging processes, evaluates their current shipping and packaging systems, and even recommends superior packaging solutions. Additionally, the site includes a handful of useful resources (articles and studies) to aid the business customer.

Sealed Air's second strategy concentrates on developing superior packaging products. Two flagship Sealed Air products are Instapak foam packaging and Bubble Wrap cushioning. Consider the Web-based firm EasyClosets.com. EasyClosets offers a Web site where a consumer interactively designs a contemporary closet using the company's modules; the company then assembles a kit of materials and ships it on order. The dilemma facing EasyClosets was that its model involved shipping closet materials directly to customers. Any damage en route not only resulted in a dissatisfied customer but also triggered an expensive return and resend cycle. By using Sealed Air's packaging products, EasyClosets reduced its packaging time from four hours to one hour and virtually eliminated damaged merchandise.

By introducing innovative products and providing clients with full packaging solutions, Sealed Air was able to exploit second-order effects of the Internet boom.

Move #23: Launch a Disruptive Response to Cycles

A final way to benefit from industry cycles is to introduce innovations that mute or eliminate the impact of cycles. This is a major driver behind the adoption of flexible manufacturing systems, in which entire factories can fairly readily be converted from the creation of one sort of output to another. Although introducing flexibility can be expensive, it reduces the pressures that lead to much dysfunctional competitive behavior in cyclical or uneven-demand industries by limiting the sunk costs of overcapacity situations and allowing firms to capture the benefits of tight-capacity ones.

Example: Creating a Production System That Is Cycle-Resistant. Electronics provider Agilysys (formerly Pioneer-Standard Electronics) has invested significantly in combining its assembly, distribution, and computer component storage operations into a new distribution and value-added center. Although many of the components of its innovation are fairly standard—such as the use of just-in-time information to route components between processes—the company's efforts are distinct in terms of its consciousness of the negative impact of cycles on its economic performance. Among the benefits it cites is the ability to build more complex units while using 20 percent fewer workers. According to Jeff Levine, the company's vice president for operations, the new system "has created a more stable workforce able to handle the peaks and valleys that come," without the need for disruptive hiring and dismissal of part-time employees or scheduling changes.[12] Among the results of the shift have been a reduction in turnaround time to three days (from the former seven to ten days), better pricing power, and far greater levels of customer satisfaction.

Prospecting Questions for
Exploiting Predictable Industry Cycles

Examine your industry's sales over at least the past decade, looking for cyclical patterns. Some industries tend to follow the business cycle. Others, such as retailing, have additional seasonal cycles, and still others, such as real estate, have much longer cycles. Your task is to identify the particular cycles that impact your industry.

With this information in mind, brainstorm answers to the following questions:

What bottlenecks are likely to occur in the cyclical peaks?

What surpluses are likely to occur in the troughs?

Are there ways to end-run swings in the industry by positioning your firm to exploit bottlenecks during peak demand and to avoid troughs?

What second-order effects will cyclical swings have on the industry?

What second-order demands or surpluses will be created? For you? For members of the industry value chain, such as suppliers and distributors?

Are there opportunities to introduce innovations that mute or eliminate the impact of cycles?

MarketBuster Prospecting During Shifts in
Industry Constraints or Barriers

It may be possible to identify marketbusting opportunities by exploiting a significant shift that has changed or will change an industry constraint or barrier. For example, in regulated industries the players often focus more on how to appease regulators than on how to compete with one another; when the regulatory climate shifts, opportunities often arise. Any major change in regulations or other legal constraints can create a marketbusting opportunity. The same thing applies to changes in technology, major social shifts, changes in transportation and distribution systems, and so on.

Move #24: Exploit Shifts in Industry Constraints or Barriers

One of the most obvious chances to create a marketbuster occurs when a fundamental change in an industry environment poses an opportunity for exploitation.

Example: Expanding from Regulated to Unregulated Parts of Your Industry. The Viridian Group PLC of Northern Ireland successfully capitalized on the deregulation of electricity through a strategy of selectively entering deregulating markets while preserving the integrity of regional electric company Northern Ireland Electricity (NIE). NIE provides power to about seven hundred thousand homes and businesses in Northern Ireland. Viridian's unregulated businesses include business process outsourcing (Sx3), financial services (Open + Direct), power marketing (Energia), and high-voltage electrical infrastructure contracting (NIE Powerteam). Its Nevada telecom joint venture with Energis provides voice, data, Internet, and e-commerce services.

Anticipating further increases in deregulation, NIE is building an underwater interconnector that will give NIE customers access to electricity from Great Britain. The company has also entered the Republic of Ireland's electricity market, which is opening up to competition. Its Energia subsidiary markets retail and wholesale electricity in the Republic of Ireland as well as Northern Ireland. Through its Huntstown Power unit, Viridian is building a gas-fired 340-megawatt power plant north of Dublin. The key point about Viridian's success is that it proactively built competencies ahead of the industry-transforming event and thus was able to move quickly when deregulation occurred. Viridian has shown steady growth in revenues, from $908 million in 2001 to $1.5 billion projected for 2004.

Example: A Failed Attempt to Capitalize on Industry-wide Changes. Such opportunities can also prove to be dangerous, however, if implementation is not carefully thought through. Indeed, the recent history of deregulated or globalizing industries from telecom to energy suggests that such conditions will tend to attract investment from many overly optimistic would-be victors. The case of the Asia Power Group's attempt to create a marketbusting strategy in the domestic energy market of the Republic of China is a cautionary tale.

The industry's prospects were set against a backdrop of dramatic domestic growth; GDP growth in the ROC exceeded 10 percent throughout most of the 1990s, with the trend expected to continue. At that time, 35 percent of homes had little or no access to electricity, and the Chinese government's own projections indicated that it would cost $500 billion to create the energy infrastructure needed to modernize the country. In response, in 1994, China changed restrictive regulations to permit foreigners to form joint ventures with provinces and municipalities to create build-operate-transfer plants. The plants were to be built by the foreign firms, operated at a price determined by the Chinese government, and then transferred to the joint venture partner. The deals were structured to be lucrative for the foreign firms, which could earn a return greater than 20 percent. So far, it sounds like a great opportunity, doesn't it?

In October 1993, three Canadian power companies—Ontario Hydro, Hydro Quebec, and Power Corporation of Canada—formed an alliance to capitalize on China's untapped energy market. The venture became known as the Asia Power Group, and its primary purpose was to invest in energy opportunities in Asia. Although the opportunities were indeed bright, the partners ended up not achieving their goals for dramatic profit growth. This was because, among other reasons, they underestimated how much competition they would encounter and overestimated how easy it would be to quickly establish themselves as trusted partners in an environment in which relationships are critical. The partnership was disbanded in 1996, with its failure attributed to divergent objectives on the part of the partners and with unexpected competition.

Example: Creating the Right Context Before You Leap In. A better example is offered by a large contract that was bid in 1996 for a 700-megawatt coal-fired plant in the Guangxi Zhuang region of southern China. A European consortium composed of Electricite de France International and GEC Alsthom won the $800 million project. The consortium had not only thought through the technical requirements for capturing the contract but had also proactively been developing strong ties with members of the Chinese government for years. Thus, although many firms saw the opportunities in China—six consortia bid on the Guangxi Zhuang project—relatively few proactively created the conditions that would allow them to capture the opportunity in a changing industry.

Move #25: Capitalize on Second-Order Effects of Shifts in Constraints

As with industry cycles, major shifts in industry constraints can create a host of second-order opportunities for those players having insight into the likely consequences. Changes in rules regarding national competition often create opportunities across many industries.

Example: Taking Advantage of Pending Changes in the Italian Insurance Market. One of our research collaborators, Clive Mendes, used insight into European Union trends in regulation to dramatically reposition personal insurance in Italy. He described it to us this way:

> *Royal Insurance was the fruit of a strategic review which I carried out in 1994 for Lloyd Italia Spa which was at the time the largest Italian subsidiary of the British Royal Insurance Group. Royal Insurance,*

like all large groups was looking out for opportunities for profitable development in its various markets. In Italy, at the time, there was a lot of changes going on in the legislative and cultural framework of the nation and I believed that an opportunity was developing to change the way personal lines insurance, particularly motor [auto] insurance was transacted.

I knew, though, that the European Union was about to require all European governments to "liberalize" their motor insurance markets. This would mean that individual companies would be free to set their own prices and conditions. I guessed at the time that most Italian companies would not be ready, after many years of simply administering a government tariff, to make a rapid transition to a more advanced, personalised form of pricing. My view was that in many cases they lacked the knowledge, they lacked the in-depth statistical analyses necessary and, most importantly, there was an inherent cultural conservatism or mindset which would make it difficult for most insurers to achieve the radical changes that would be necessary in the short term. They would get there eventually, but, in the meantime, there would be a few years for a creative first-mover to re-draw the playing field.

Mendes set about creating an entirely different kind of insurance company in Italy, capitalizing on the second-order effects of the deregulation trend and his parent company's sophisticated capabilities. He created the first direct distribution model for insurance in Italy, emphasized customer satisfaction in an industry in which that had not been a primary criterion, and also leveraged his company's capabilities of insurance risk analysis and operations. In January 2002, Royal Insurance was purchased for £12 million by Direct Line.

A somewhat more diffuse trend than shifting regulation, but one that creates enormous second-order opportunity, has to do with the emergence of new concepts or even fads. One example was the emergence of the concept of "best practice" study for major corporations in the early 1980s.

Example: The Corporate Executive Board Capitalizes on the Hunger for Companies to Compare Themselves to Other Companies. Corporate Executive Board (CEB) created an entire business model around the concept of benchmarking. David Bradley, CEB's founder, started the company in 1979 to do esoteric business research. That didn't work very well, but in the course of pursuing this business, CEB developed the concept of keeping companies from reinventing the wheel every time they have a problem.

Now CEB collects solutions to various business problems from its large corporate customers. Relevant problems might include boosting employee retention or minimizing government regulatory costs. It then assembles this management wisdom, adds its own insights, compiles it all into reports, and sells it to subscribers, which are usually other large corporations. This model has worked so well that it has placed CEB into "hot growth" company lists of both *Business Week* and *Fortune*.[13] From 1998 to 2000, revenues grew at an average annual pace of 35 percent, and profit growth averaged 153 percent annually. CEB's average return on capital over those years was 61.4 percent. CEB's stock, a split-adjusted $9.50 at initial public offering in 1999, recently closed at $33.

Move #26: Use a Shift in a Key Constraint to Disrupt the Industry

Often, an industrywide shift can be traced to the emergence of a technological innovation that changes customer expectations. Sometimes directly, sometimes indirectly, new ways of doing things can send ripples across an entire industry and dramatically shift the power dynamics within it. New approaches can also cause the stable structure of an industry to fragment, making room for smaller players or players with different strategies.

Example: Allergan Creates a Revolution in Wrinkle Treatment. Allergan, founded in 1951, is a California-based niche provider of health care solutions for neuromuscular skin and eye care. The company's initial product, an antihistamine eye drop called Allergan, was its first innovation. Its growth (greater than 20 percent annual revenue growth for much of its history) continued to be driven by innovative solutions in niche markets, primarily in eye care in the early stages. In 1988, Allergan acquired the rights to a botulinum toxin product called Oculinum, which would later evolve into a product called Botox.

Botox is a purified protein toxin derived from clostridium botulinum bacteria. In the late 1970s, researchers used small amounts of Botox to treat muscle disorders such as facial twitching and muscle spasms, and in 1989 the Food and Drug Administration (FDA) approved Botox for the treatment of eye muscle disorders. In the same year, a Canadian professor using Botox to treat a patient with eyelid muscle twitching noticed that the wrinkles around the area improved, and that sparked a revolution in the world of cosmetic treatment.

Cosmetic specialists have since aggressively marketed Botox to their clientele as an alternative to surgery. What the clients don't necessarily realize is how much business sense it makes for providers to use Botox rather than perform surgery. Surgery requires high malpractice insurance, a longer procedure, and a longer recovery period. Since surgery is permanent, patients seldom repeat their visits. Botox, in contrast, is not permanent, so patients come back. It's also not covered by Medicare or most insurance plans, so patients who want the treatment pay in advance. Rather than wait around for reimbursement, doctors have the cash in hand immediately. Doctors get between $400 and $1,000 per patient every three to four months for a five-minute procedure. In addition, doctors recover the cost of the vial on the first patient because Allergan charges $400 for a vial that will treat five patients. Moreover, patients are released thirty minutes to two hours after the procedure, increasing patient turnaround.

From the consumer's point of view, Botox offers a minimally invasive procedure that is cost effective, painless, and convenient.

Prospecting Questions for Exploiting Shifts in Industry Constraints or Barriers

List the most important constraints or barriers that have bounded the competition in your industry. Identify those that are or likely will be under pressure to change. Brainstorm those constraints and barriers for answers to the following questions:

Is there a way of capitalizing on this shift by exploiting the new competitive opportunities that it creates?

What are the second-order effects that this shift will create in your industry? In the value chain that supports it?

Can you exploit these second-order effects by making a market-busting move?

Can you exploit this shift to disrupt the way competitors compete?

Patients avoid spending time in an expensive hospital bed recuperating from invasive surgery. The convenience of the treatment is a key attribute. To paraphrase one consumer, "Getting a Botox shot takes less time than a haircut." The treatment requires virtually no effort on the part of the consumer aside from the commute to the physician's office. The treatment shows results immediately, as opposed to surgery, which requires a convalescence period. Botox sales are projected to grow at 20 to 30 percent per year for the next few years, and Allergan's Botox revenues are projected to reach $808 million by 2005.[14]

MarketBuster Prospecting to Exploit Industry Evolution

Like products, industries go through several life cycle stages, beginning with early experimentation, continuing through growth and maturity, and finally ending up in a slow- or no-growth endgame of decline.[15] Preparing for the evolution of an industry allows the insightful firm to stake out positions that can convey intriguing advantages as the industry matures. Research has consistently identified certain patterns. They include the predominance of product innovation in the early days of an industry, with process innovation becoming more prominent as it matures; the tendency of maturing industries to undergo consolidation; and the tendency for the products offered in mature industries to become commoditized.[16]

Marketbusting opportunities emerge for those firms that anticipate life cycle trends in product categories, such as the transition from feature innovations to process innovations. Manufacturers of mobile telephones, for example, have shifted from innovating in features and attributes to innovating in fashion and services. Mike Zafirovski is president and chief operating officer of Motorola, Inc. When Zafirovski was president of Motorola's personal communications sector, he redesigned both the products and the manufacturing system to anticipate this industry trend. Previously, the company had offered many phone models that required various hardware and software parts. With the design of the newer models, Motorola's phones had 40 to 45 percent of their parts in common at the end of 2001 compared with the previous 10 to 20 percent.

Move #27: Exploit Your Industry's Structure for the Next Life Cycle Stage

One pattern of exploiting evolutionary industry paths is an industry roll-up. Roll-up involves consolidating some aspect of the value chains of a fragmented industry. A familiar example is the invasion of big box retailers into industry segments that were formerly occupied by mom-and-pop small businesses. Office suppliers such as Staples and Office Max, huge home entertainment stores such as Circuit City and HMV, and home improvement centers such as Lowe's and The Home Depot have all employed a variant of the defragmenting strategy.

By exploiting volume, technological, and pricing advantages, these retailers are able to provide goods at much more competitive prices than their smaller rivals can achieve. Although their service tends to be less personal than that in a locally owned shop, for many items customers simply don't care. Instead, the variety, long hours, low prices, and selection offered by the large suppliers creates real value for the customer.

Of course, the conditions under which a roll-up will succeed are not infinite. There must be enough underserved customers to merit the investment, and the differentiation offered by a superstore must be sufficiently compelling to persuade customers to change their shopping habits. In the U.K., for example, entrepreneurs tried to copy The Home Depot's model with DIY (do it yourself) stores in the 1980s. Unfortunately, even though smaller competitors were driven out of business in large numbers, too many large chains entered, trying to chase too few customers on price competition alone. Only when retailer Boots entered did competition shift from price to differentiation, product variety, and customer service.[17]

Another example and a bit of a cautionary tale is Service Corporation International (SCI). Hoover's online Web site (www.hoovers.com) observes that "SCI is to death what H&R Block is to taxes." SCI is the largest funeral company in the world. It owns 3,125 funeral homes, cemeteries, crematoria, and flower shops in eleven countries, primarily in the United States and Canada. Robert Waltrip, the author of the company's current strategy, inherited the business at the age of twenty in the early 1950s. He decided to grow the funeral business by mimicking the growth strategies of service companies such as Holiday Inn and McDonald's. This unconventional strategy allowed SCI to grow (primarily through acquisition), even though the conventional wisdom at the time was that the funeral business could never be national because of local ties, local regulations, and the highly personal nature of the business.

By colocating its facilities (funeral homes, florist shops, and so on), SCI shares personnel, vehicles, and preparation services, making it possible for it to operate more cost effectively than competitors having only one location. SCI has also preserved the individual nature of the businesses it bought in order to remain a trusted source for different religious and ethnic groups.

SCI has also taken advantage of some other techniques for marketbusting. It changed the payment stream in its industry, for example, by allowing customers to purchase funerals in advance, thus locking in preinflationary prices. SCI's 2001 sales totaled $2.5 billion, and it has arranged future business of $4.6 billion in prepaid funeral contracts.

Growth has not been without its difficulties. Accusations of poor management of some funeral operations and overly ambitious international acquisitions have been troublesome in recent years. In addition, the spending by the company to pursue its acquisition-oriented growth strategy has left it burdened with debt at a time when trends are going against it. Nonetheless, the performance of the company in what may well be the ultimate mature industry has been historically remarkable.

Move #28: Understand the Second-Order Effects of the Next Stage

In developing industries it's common for vertically integrated companies to exit certain noncore businesses as the industry matures. This is particularly true of high-technology businesses, which find it extremely difficult to remain at the state of the art in every technological aspect of the industry compared with players that focus on only one.[18]

Example: DuPont Creates Efficiencies by Specializing in Photomasks. DuPont capitalized on the second-order effects of industry development with its photomask offerings. Photomasks are quartz or glass plates that are used to etch microscopic circuitry onto semiconductor wafers. Several years ago, chip manufacturers (Intel, Texas Instruments, and so on) would have their own photomask divisions transfer their chip design onto their chips. However, technology for photomasking equipment rapidly improved, and costs for making, inspecting, and repairing the equipment skyrocketed from the low seven figures to $10 million and up. Chip manufacturers began to focus on their core competency of making chips and not masks, creating the opportunity for DuPont to acquire masking operations of major chip manufacturers. DuPont's strategy has allowed the firm to integrate its operations into those of the chip manufacturers and also grow its revenues substantially. In 2000, DuPont Photomasks, Inc., saw revenues grow almost 25 percent, from $264 million in 1999 to $328.1 million in 2000.[19]

Move #29: Redirect, Disrupt, or Alter the Evolutionary Trajectory

When an industry has reached a certain level of maturity, many of the characteristics of its offerings become standardized. In the language of attribute mapping (see chapter 3), the offerings acquire a great many nonnegotiables, and it becomes more difficult to introduce new exciters or differentiators. Standardization, however, offers several benefits. It becomes easier to communicate what an industry's offerings are, and as customers gain experience there is less need for continual education and training. In addition, many activities can become routine, and thus players avoid the need to invent processes from scratch.

But a subtle vulnerability can become manifest among leaders in a mature industry: As their offerings become increasingly standardized, new entrants may seek to divert that stable trajectory by creating a disruptive offering. *Disruptive offerings*, in the sense coined by Clayton Christensen, are those that appeal to a different (often less demanding) user set or are cheaper, simpler, or less complex for new groups of users to adopt.[20] They are disruptive because incumbents seldom see the threat coming. New entrants often compete in places and with vehicles that are not readily visible, often because they grow in product or market environments that the incumbents have not addressed. If the upstart succeeds, the incremental evolution of an industry can again change to one of flux.

Example: Ticketmaster Versus Tickets.com. Ticketmaster is the dominant player in the ticketing industry, with approximately 80 percent of the market. Ticketmaster fully handles the ticketing needs of venues, but at a hefty price per ticket. The cost of the service includes staffing call centers, taking online sales, selling at box offices, and processing ticket fulfillment, in addition to other services at events. For these services, Ticketmaster receives, on average, $7 per ticket.

Tickets.com offers a cheaper alternative. One of the most important distinctions between Ticketmaster and Tickets.com is the latter's dual product offering. In addition to the commonplace ticket-selling and distribution services, Tickets.com offers software that allows clients to control their own ticketing programs in-house. By simplifying the ticketing program and giving control to the venues, Tickets.com allows them to run their own ticketing operations and thereby save money compared with the cost of the Ticketmaster package of services.

Tickets.com offers three main software products for in-house ticketing: Prologue, Pass3 for Windows, and TicketMaker Professional. All three products offer significant telephone support and the option to purchase additional integrated modules. Furthermore, the products are tailored for venues of various sizes. One can anticipate that Tickets.com's tailored offerings for smaller venues will be particularly disruptive, because these clients are often overlooked by major ticketing providers.

Tickets.com has set its sights on unseating Ticketmaster as the leading ticketing service provider and disrupting the evolution of ticketing services. Tickets.com was founded in 1996 and went public in the heady days of 1999. Over the three months ended May 31, 2002, total revenues rose 20 percent, to $17.9 million. Although it is not yet clear that Tickets.com will prevail, it provides a useful illustration of an attempt to shake up a settled industry by disrupting at the low end.

Prospecting Questions for Exploiting Industry Evolution

Examine the evolution of your product life cycle, and identify the ways competitors have converged in the current stage of the industry's evolution. Look for indicators that this convergence is vulnerable to a competitive format that will move the industry into the next life cycle stage. Have your team begin to probe whether there are opportunities to capitalize on life cycle shifts:

Are there places (proliferation of product models, emergence of dominant design, preemptive roll-up, or consolidation) where you can anticipate and capture first-mover advantages by preemptive evolutionary moves?

Can you anticipate second-order effects of industry evolution by pinpointing places where industry fragmentation, disintermediation, or concentration creates marketbusting opportunities?

Are there ways you might be able to move boldly to redirect, alter, or disrupt the current course of the industry?

MarketBuster Prospecting When the Value Chain Shifts

The final industry pattern we have observed to be a source of opportunity arises when something changes, causing shifts in the structure of existing value chains. Unlike the often dramatic changes that influence an industry by shifting a constraint or regulatory barrier as discussed earlier, the changes here refer to innovations that ease bottlenecks or reduce costs. These innovations can also affect existing value chains by adding new components to them or by decreasing the value of or need for certain portions of the chains.

Move #30: Exploit a Shift in the Value Chain

One way to make money in these circumstances is to capture control of resources that are suddenly more scarce, expensive, or important than before, or to innovate to reduce the scarcity, cost, or importance of those resources. One approach is to automate, routinize, or standardize processes that were once complex and required high levels of skills. What happens then is that the control of the value chain shifts to some other component.

Example: Standardizing Construction Elements to Radically Reduce Cost. BT Building Systems is a Connecticut-based company that creates preassembled walls to specifications provided by its customers. The key value for customers is leverage: Rather than build framing for a construction job on-site using skilled workers, BT's system uses specialized computer-aided design and computer-aided manufacturing (CAD/CAM) techniques to create walls in a factory setting.

Although the CAD/CAM system is complex and expensive (as of this writing, only four companies offer a similar process), after the process is running at scale BT can offer customers significant advantages compared with the old approach. For one thing, weather and other on-site impediments don't delay the schedule. In addition, the system can kick in when needed, avoiding the inefficiencies of unpredictable construction schedules. And of course, builders using the system require fewer highly skilled framers on-site, something that saves cost and increases flexibility. Initial customers are expected to be those for whom cost is a major consideration (such as low-income housing projects), but after the technology improves it has the potential to influence the entire value chain of the building and construction business. BT's senior executives passionately believe that as many as 80 percent of future construction sites will use this technology.

Example: Importing and Exporting Business Methods from One Environment to Another. Value chain shifts can also occur when firms with origins in different institutional environments seek to expand, thus changing the value chains in their target arenas. South African Breweries (SAB) enjoyed a dominant position (98 percent market share) in the beer business in South Africa. Apartheid prevented SAB from making overseas investments throughout the 1980s, leading it to diversify in domestic businesses. For many years, export restrictions and international disapproval limited its ability to expand, and volatile economic conditions and home and currency instability forced the company to become an extremely efficient operator. Then in the early 1990s, sanctions against South African companies were lifted. SAB's management decided that its lean operating model could dramatically change value chains in the international beer business, and the firm set about expanding globally.

SAB now has major operations in Africa, China, India, Central Europe, and Central America. One of its most visible recent acquisitions was the 2002 purchase of Miller Brewing to create SABMiller PLC, making the new company the world's second-largest brewer. In what others might consider a mature market, SABMiller produced 23.5 percent net income growth in 2002 on the basis of only 3.6 percent growth in sales—clear evidence of its ability to make the entire value chain in which it operates more efficient.

Firms seeking to exploit a shift in the value chain can also use a strategy that we term *linchpin alliance.* You can use this approach when your firm has developed capabilities that have very wide application potential and that you can license or sell to be incorporated into the products of a large number of alliance partners for whom the capability delivers a critical functionality. The market-busting opportunity is to create alliances with all the beneficiaries of your capability and end up as the linchpin.

Move #31: Exploit Second-Order Effects of Shifts in the Value Chain

Strong trends or step changes are another major cue to begin probing and thinking about second-order causes and consequences of the dynamics of your current view of the world. So if you are experiencing or riding a trend it might be insightful to ask, "What trend (or change) could be causing this trend?" or "What trend (or change) could this trend cause?" Then begin to think through the opportunities that might flow from this.

Example: Turning Sand into a Valuable Scarce Commodity. An entrepreneur we know learned of the pending development of a huge open cast copper mining project in the African bush. He pursued the following line of logic: "To build a huge mine in the bush will require the development of housing for the workers and roads, buildings, and bridges for the mine and township. To build houses, buildings, roads, and bridges will require megatons of concrete. To make concrete will require megatons of sand. Transporting sand is very expensive." So he drew a 100-mile circle around the proposed site, went to all the farmers who owned river property in that circle, and took out options on the rights to their river sand. Then he sat and waited for people needing sand to mix into their concrete. Eventually, they found him and he was able to lock in a generous profit from the sales of a commodity product that was suddenly scarce.

The kinds of opportunities to look for here are chances to eliminate gaps or glitches in existing value chains, to attain a position of power in a reconfigured value chain, or to help customers and clients maneuver in reconfigured value chains.

Example: Helping Customers Respond to Value Chain Upheavals. SAP is a premier provider of enterprise resource planning (ERP) software, which lets different parts of an organization, as well as other parties in its value chain, work from the same information, which is kept in common formats. The underlying need for such systems is often caused by value chain or competitive pressures that threaten the configuration of existing supply relations in an industry.

Recently, for example, German pharmaceutical manufacturer Bayer AG encountered an extraordinary spike in demand for its Cipro product, an antibiotic, stemming from the discovery of anthrax-tainted letters sent to victims in Florida, Maryland, New Jersey, New York, Virginia, and Washington, D.C. Historically, pharmaceutical manufacturing has been a process of forecasting demand and then manufacturing in batches to meet demand by carrying inventories; the same production plants are used for different products and must be certified for the manufacture of only that product for each production run. Coping with the unexpected demand for Cipro led Bayer to assign nonmanufacturing personnel to factories, to allow around-the-clock manufacturing, and to initiate arduous communications by telephone, e-mail, and fax to make sure that other value chain partners (particularly suppliers, wholesalers, and large pharmacy chains) were coordinated.[21]

Such experiences have created second-order demand for ERP systems such as those made by SAP. With an ERP-type system, organizations can quickly detect and address shortages and glitches. In addition, the system can provide the capacity to rapidly run alternative scenarios and help its clients develop the most appropriate response in an automated manner. Ultimately such systems have the potential for creating a competitive edge for companies that use them and a disadvantage for companies that don't. As Garnet Group analyst French Caldwell recently observed, what drives demand for systems such as SAP's is "to have better insight and be able to integrate the data it's getting from inventory and supply chain management and from market and business intelligence with internal intelligence to improve its product development process." The long-term bottlenecks addressed by systems such as SAP's are those that affect product development time.

Move #32: Reduce Costs or Abolish Bottlenecks to Disrupt the Value Chain

Often, existing ways of competing coincide with existing value chains. When there is a shift, you may be able to benefit from the instability in a value chain to improve your position with respect to the rest of the industry. Your industry may, for example, have settled into relatively predictable patterns of competition. Such strategic lockstep occurs when competition has been dominated for some time by a few, largely identical providers competing in much the same way. An opportunity may exist for a new competitive model to be introduced by a marketbuster that the incumbents are reluctant to copy.

Example: The Explosive Growth of Affinity Cards. Started in 1982, MBNA uses affinity programs in which organizations endorse its credit cards. In exchange, MBNA imprints the organizations' logos on the cards and gives them a percentage of the revenues generated. Through such partnerships, MBNA has created an earnings juggernaut, with $98 billion in loans, 15 percent of the U.S. credit card market, and the second-lowest rate of bad loans in the industry.

MBNA began its business by focusing on high-quality professional groups through trade shows, telemarketing, and direct mail. The company increased its market share of low-risk card users and concentrates almost exclusively on upper-market, free-spending borrowers. MBNA banks on customers to carry a balance from month to month in order to make money from interest payments.

Because of MBNA's rigorous screening process, the company keeps its credit card loss rate below the industry's average. In 2001, the company wrote off only 4.7 percent of its loans, well below the industry average of 6.9 percent. Its screening process includes computer models, and a person reviews every account. MBNA's low-risk customer base has also helped the company to weather the weak economy better than most creditors.

With four thousand seven hundred affiliate organizations, MBNA has become a credit card giant, with annual earnings gains of 25 percent or more for the past nine years. MBNA is also moving its operations into Canada and Europe, where it has almost two hundred member corporations.[22]

Example: Kinder Morgan Energy Partners. In 1997 Richard Kinder and William Morgan paid $40 million for Enron Liquids Pipeline, L.P. At the time, the conventional wisdom was that the oil and gas pipeline and storage industry was profitable but slow growing. Kinder, a former Enron executive, saw a huge opportunity by rethinking the way business was done in the industry. He left Enron to form Kinder Morgan Energy Partners, L.P. By cutting $5 million in costs, largely by eliminating headquarters staff, the company increased cash flow and boosted the dividends to the limited partners by more than 50 percent in less than six months.

Kinder Morgan's pipelines move gasoline, diesel, jet fuel, and natural gas from petroleum refineries to regional markets and can do this with dependable revenues. The company has more than thirty thousand miles of pipeline. Kinder Morgan also operates some thirty-three bulk terminals that handle 55 million tons of materials such as coal and petroleum coke. By accumulating pipelines and terminals, the company has acquired the assets that are central to the energy infrastructure of growing markets.

Kinder Morgan has also leveraged its Master Limited Partnership (MLP) financial structure, which allows it to capitalize on tax advantages. The company pays no corporate income tax as long as it distributes most of its earnings as dividends. It also avoids the double taxation of dividends that most companies face. As a result, its entire pretax earnings go to shareholders, whereas most companies would endure federal, state, and local governments skimming off 40 percent or more of that earnings stream. Kinder explains the advantage: "When I was president of Enron, I would have thrown people out of the room if they came in with a proposal that had anything

Prospecting Questions for Reordering or Relocating Your Space on the Value Chain

Examine the value chain of your industry, reviewing how it has changed and how its value-capture patterns are shifting. Use your insights to seek marketbusting opportunities to capture value or relocate your participation at emergent shifts in the chain:

Can you spot places to exploit shifts that are occurring or will occur in the value chain structure?

Can you pinpoint second-order consequences up and down the chain where you can reposition your participation?

Can you spot places where you can disrupt the current value chain and change it in ways that suit you?

less than a 15% aftertax return. We can make acquisitions all day as long as we're over 8.5% pretax."

Since its formation in 1997, Kinder Morgan has grown through acquisitions of pipelines and terminals, including a $1.4 billion acquisition of Santa Fe Pacific Pipelines and a $1.15 billion purchase of the U.S. terminals and pipeline assets of GATX Corp. The company has also grown through expansion projects.

Kinder Morgan's sales (in millions of dollars) were 323, 429, 816, and 2,947 in 1998, 1999, 2000, and 2001, respectively.[23]

Action Steps for Exploiting Industry Shifts

Step 1: With your strategy team, use the questions in table 5-1 to determine whether there is evidence that some kinds of dynamic changes are occurring at an industry level. Depending on the evidence, conduct the analyses we suggest for the specific pattern. There may be evidence that more than one pattern change is under way or imminent. So much the better! What you are trying to figure out is whether there are early indicators of the opportunities created by transforming industries.

Step 2: If you have concluded that there may be opportunities at an industry level, apply the prospecting questions that we suggest for each level to see whether there is a chance to make one of three possible moves:

- Can you capture an advantage because you are among the first to spot and exploit a new pattern of industry change?

- What are the likely second-order effects of a change that is clearly occurring? Can you capitalize on these?

- Are you in a position to disrupt or provoke a change in the industry?

Step 3: For those ideas you deem to be most attractive, put together a short feasibility overview. What are the main assumptions you are making about how you will succeed? What are the skills and competencies you must have for this to work? What is the step-by-step path forward?

Step 4: Consider the timing and implementation challenges of executing a strategy for exploiting industry shifts.

6

EXPLOIT EMERGING OPPORTUNITIES

Up to this point, this book has dealt primarily with existing markets and industries having reasonably definable boundaries. In this chapter, we examine those rare instances in which significant changes have led to the creation of entirely new markets or industries. We shift from looking at customers, segments, and industries to looking at the dynamics that sometimes lead to major shifts in needs, which in turn can lead to major opportunities.

Chapter 5 looked at forces that affect all players in an industry—you and your competition together. The issues we explored there had to do with exploiting more or less regular trends and cycles at an industry level. In this chapter, we talk about opportunities that emerge when a confluence of shifting factors comes together to create an entirely different strategic landscape from the one you have been working with. If chapter 5 was about capitalizing on dynamics you see first, this one is about anticipating a phase change in the competitive environment.

The metaphor we like to use to describe these sorts of shifts is that of a tectonic plate shift. Tectonic plates lie under the earth's continents and are constantly in motion. A tectonic plate shift occurs when numerous small things accumulate to reach a breaking point. What is interesting about tectonic plate shifts in economies is that their advent often can be anticipated. It's also interesting that the rise of a new industry usually benefits new firms that form around the opportunities it represents, and not established firms, even though one might think that the latter have the competencies and skills to take advantage of them.[1]

Creating Customers: What Works?

First, let's acknowledge that few established firms become successful quickly in brand-new markets and industries. The very practices that go together with long-term reliable success tend to be inimical to success in new environments.[2] In a few cases, however, companies have pulled it off, and their stories represent the last class of marketbusters that we address in this book.

Some market creation is driven by the vision of a person at the top—often the CEO, although not always. Occasionally, the vision actually provokes the changes that lead to a major industry shift. Steve Jobs at Apple is justifiably famous for envisioning whole new market spaces—not just once, as with the personal computer, but repeatedly, both successfully and unsuccessfully. His wildly successful company Pixar, for example, was formed to capitalize on the development of digital media animation, whereas his NeXT computer (an early PDA) was a disappointment. Most recently, Jobs's Apple Computer has developed devices to take advantage of the emergence of the "digital jukebox" for music. Unfortunately, individual genius is hard to reproduce with any reliability.

Behavior that requires a little less overwhelming insight, but that does require senior intervention, is to identify a tectonic shift and mobilize the company to go after it. A well-known example is Microsoft's about-face on the importance of the Internet after the company initially dismissed its significance.

Another, albeit unreliable, vehicle for capitalizing on industry change is called *slack search* by academics.[3] In this method, you create free resources at the operating level, resources that empower employees to explore interesting opportunities in a relatively undirected way. Unfortunately, this frequently used method is unpredictable and often unsuccessful. Often, such groups are not given sufficient time, cannot integrate with the parent organization, end up being eliminated during cost cutting, or otherwise become regarded as expensive deviants by their parent organizations. A variant of this strategy is to pursue new spaces through partnerships, such as strategic alliances or industry consortia. Similar risks pertain. Tools that we have sometimes seen such groups use to good effect are scenario planning, heavyweight internal champions, and various forms of exploratory sense-making.[4]

Another practice that can prove fruitful is to follow the entrepreneurs. Look at where start-ups are entering and use their activities as a cue to do likewise, or use corporate venture capital to provide a window on interesting developments. Or you can buy a partial stake in a smaller company. Similarly, you might consider building partnerships with universities and other centers of innovation.[5]

Sometimes an established firm causes a new market to emerge purely on the basis of its own clout. Perhaps the most famous historical example is the way in which IBM's entry into the personal computer market created an alternative standard to the Apple II overnight and established a market that—although nascent with

---

Why It Is Hard to Capitalize on New Markets

When envisioning new markets, companies often make a number of critical mistakes. First, because the shift that represents the emergence of an opportunity is often small, they may not see the trend as significant. Even Microsoft missed the early signs that the Internet would become significant. More frequently, existing players are wedded to an alternative solution that would be threatened by a major change. RCA, for example, failed to capitalize on transistors because it was dependent on vacuum tubes and didn't try to take advantage of the emerging opportunity.[6] Sometimes, the change is so threatening that established industries seek to fight it. Consider the music labels' history of fighting every successive wave of new technology in that industry, from 33-rpm albums to the advent of downloadable music. Sometimes companies move too early. The personal digital assistant market, for example, saw dozens of hopeful firms enter and exit before the PDA finally became a mass-market product.

To see a tectonic plate shift coming, you must put together many bits of seemingly uncorrelated and sometimes seemingly unimportant information. When we are scanning and gathering intelligence to keep an existing business going, rarely do we fine-tune our activities to spot evidence that a new business may be emerging.

It is also hard to see the utility of a new solution before it has been experienced. Market research won't tell you very much about a market that doesn't yet exist. Until a certain amount of cumulative marketplace experimentation has built up, it's hard to see what the real opportunities will be.[7] The difficulty is that if you take on the burden of doing all that experimentation, there is no guarantee that your firm will reap the rewards; after you have demonstrated that an opportunity exists, others can easily follow your lead and capture the benefits.[8]

Further, new markets often start small and fall into market segments that are not considered mainstream.[9] That makes them hard to spot, because again no amount of market research that reflects your current understanding of who is buying your offerings will help you understand customers that you don't serve in markets that it never occurred to you to approach. Why did the Victor Talking Machine Company not dominate radio, and why did existing watchmakers miss the emergence of electronic watches? The reason is that the customers for those new products were a different group from those served by these companies, so they couldn't use existing customers and needs as a guide to where best to innovate.

Apple's innovation—grew rapidly only after IBM made a commitment to it. As of this writing, Intel is attempting a similar move in the world of wireless communication chips for laptop computers, IBM is seeking to create a market for "on demand" computing, and companies such as America Online are seeking to develop a market for "bring your own access" Internet experiences.

Foreseeing a New Market: The Tectonic Triggers Table

As with chapter 5, where we discussed the forces that can lead an industry to dramatically change, here we are concerned with those forces that can lead to the emergence of a new market.[10] Economist Leon Walras long ago articulated the fundamental source of value in an economy as the combination of utility and scarcity.[11] In considering whether a new industry might be emerging, we are looking for shifts in perceptions of utility (usefulness, desirability) among large groups of potential customers, and shifts in the scarcity (or uniqueness) of solutions.

If value is created because an offering addresses some need or want, a logical question is, what causes needs to change? To answer this question, you'll need to look at longer-term trends and changes in the environment. Some companies have a formal process for doing this, such as the famous scenario planning group developed by Royal Dutch Shell, the use of macro-trend studies by DuPont, or the reports issued by the Institute for the Future for its consortium clients. Essentially, these techniques call for firms to look at sets of correlated possibilities to envision possible futures.

Firms such as these study situations in which a change in technology enables new solutions that formerly were not possible. New drugs, for example, create markets by allowing treatment for disease states that previously were not addressable. The Internet allows e-mail communication to operate asynchronously, speeding up written communication and in many cases replacing verbal communication.

As with the second-order effects of industry trends discussed in chapter 5, technological progress often leads to second-order problems. These are often counterintuitive, seeming to obey the law of unintended consequences. Thus, we see Xerox copiers that are so advanced that counterfeiters use them to copy currency. Making cars theftproof through radio-controlled keys increases the incidence of both carjacking and key-seeking burglary. The prevalence of cellular phones provokes countermeasures to render them unworkable in environments such as hospitals, restaurants, and theaters. It has also led to a shrinking market for conventional pay telephones. Legitimate antiterrorism measures create risks to privacy, which are sure to provoke still more innovations that seek to disable those same measures.

Other trends might include changes in social possibilities. The emergence of working women and widespread international travel have created a myriad of new opportunities, from franchised day care to frequent flier programs. The two world wars introduced massive shifts in social behavior and markets. The terrorist attacks of September 11, 2001, have created vast changes in the way companies operate and in the technologies they deploy to maintain safe and secure facilities. Demographic changes are interesting, too (and are often predictable).[12]

Changes in nature also provoke new needs. Global warming, the advent of new diseases such as AIDS and SARS, and even shifts in weather patterns can create new types of demand. Another source of change concerns institutions, such as government regulations, trade barriers, tariffs, tax laws, and myriad rules of the game.

Table 6-1 summarizes these forms of triggers for a tectonic plate shift.

These major types of trends illustrate the ways in which markets can change quite fundamentally. We don't purport to offer a primer on scenario or trend analysis.[13] Still, we suggest you give some thought to these questions:

TABLE 6-1

Tectonic Triggers

Type of Trend or Shift	Definition	Examples
Technological solution	An invention or series of inventions changes what is technically feasible or affordable, creating new opportunities.	Most significant new inventions, from motorcars to airplanes to new communications devices to air conditioning and elevators.
Social possibilities and attitudes	A change in social norms and attitudes manifests itself in shifts in behavior.	Antismoking campaigns make the habit less acceptable and attractive, leading to bans on smoking in many different environments (e.g., offices, airplanes), and creating demand for antismoking assistance.
Natural phenomena	Change in some aspect of nature.	Diseases (such as AIDS and SARS), droughts, global warming, natural disasters, and other major natural changes always create business opportunities.
Institutional and regulatory change	Regulations, taxes, or other rules of law change, reorienting the structure of incentives to various commercial activities.	Deregulation of trade barriers creates opportunities for globally distributed manufacturing; deregulation of industries (airlines, banking, energy) creates massive shifts in investment and innovation.
Demographics	Changes in the proportions of different kinds of populations create increases and decreases in demand for various offerings.	Increasing numbers of middle-aged and older people drive demand for certain types of health care (for example, Viagra).

- What is your process for developing a point of view about future trends?

- Do you pay enough attention to changes that might create substantial opportunities?

- Is your point of view about the future communicated to and integrated with the people leading your innovation process?

Three Ways of Organizing Trend Analysis for MarketBuster Prospecting

Assuming that you have a process in place for assessing trends that might be important, the next step is to determine whether some kind of significant opportunity might be emerging. To do this, we propose to focus on three simple ideas.

First, consider the need you might address. Needs can be either longstanding or the new result of a major tectonic shift, so we categorize them as either existing or new. Sometimes great opportunities emerge from new solutions to old problems, whereas at other times the need itself is new. Each of the two categories has its own strategic implications.

Second, what solution might address the need? Again, the solution might call on capabilities or competencies you have already developed (perhaps in solving some other need), or it could be new. In general, it is easier and less risky to create a solution based on at least some capabilities you already have.

Finally, you'll need to consider the adequacy of existing alternative solutions. Ironically, the perceived adequacy of existing solutions to particular needs can often open an opportunity to develop a new need category, as Christensen has often pointed out. These opportunities can be remarkably fruitful for entrepreneurs, because they are not necessarily obvious to other potential new entrants.

Assessing these constructs can give you an idea of whether you might have an opportunity in a rapidly growing market space. Putting together various combinations of the three constructs allows you to develop a typology of potential opportunity types and understand what it takes to be successful in each one. The result is eight potential market-busting moves, as summarized in table 6-2 and listed here (continuing the numbering as before, to bring us to our complete set of forty moves).

Move #33: Shift the dimension of merit

Move #34: Create a market via cautious evangelism

Move #35: Build a better mousetrap

TABLE 6-2

Eight Marketbusting Moves to Exploit Emerging Opportunities

Tectonic Type	Need or Problem (existing or emerging)	Your Proposed Solution (existing or new)	Adequacy of Existing Attempts to Solve Problem
Move #33: Shift the dimension of merit	Existing	Known	Adequate
Move #34: Create a market via cautious evangelism	Existing	Known	Inadequate
Move #35: Build a better mousetrap	Existing	New	Adequate
Move #36: Undertake inventive missionary work	Existing	New	Inadequate
Move #37: Make a land grab	Emerging	Known	Adequate
Move #38: Create a niche to win	Emerging	Known	Inadequate
Move #39: Run the arms race	Emerging	New	Adequate
Move #40: Bet on blue sky ventures	Emerging	New	Inadequate

Move #36: Undertake inventive missionary work

Move #37: Make a land grab

Move #38: Create a niche to win

Move #39: Run the arms race

Move #40: Bet on Blue Sky Ventures

Before we go into these eight opportunities in more detail, we would like to set up the generic prospecting questions associated with tectonic shifts. Then we will take a close look at the challenges associated with each type of opportunity.

Addressing Tectonic Shifts

In a brainstorming session, gather evidence of key trends that might prove relevant to your position in your industry. You will want to pay particular attention to trends that are relevant to the types of tectonic pressures described in table 6-1. See whether these pressures are also beginning to create pressures in other industries. Specify your best guesses as to what changes will have to be made in the current industry offerings to cope with these pressures, and what kinds of skills and capabilities will be needed to deliver these changed offerings. Now categorize the suggested changes in terms of the typology in table 6-2.

After you identify the relevant pattern for your idea, examine the following discussion of the pattern and put together a strategy that addresses its challenges. For instance, in many industries, the confluence of aging populations, aging infrastructure, and internationalization will dramatically influence demand for such products as medical devices, elevators and escalators, and remote monitoring and communication equipment.

Move #33: Shift a Dimension of Merit

As shown in table 6-2, this move has the following pattern:

- An existing need

- Known solutions

- An adequate current solution

This category of opportunities represents situations in which a firm can prompt a tectonic shift by going beyond the solutions that have so far been offered for well-understood needs. The question is whether your proposed solution not only addresses the original needs that created the industry or market but also appeals to some new or different need that lies dormant in light of the existing solutions. The question is whether customer satisfaction along an old standard of comparison—or as the academics sometimes say, a *dimension of merit*—might lead customers to look for the next big thing.[14]

Example: Healthy, but Fast, Food. Subway is a chain of fast-food restaurants. In a departure from most of its industry peers, Subway focuses on exploiting the concept of healthy fast food. Although the problem of obesity has long been with us, in most of the developed world it has reached epidemic proportions. In the United States, for example, the past twenty years have seen a dramatic increase in obesity. Currently, more than half of all U.S. adults are considered overweight (defined as having a body mass index of 25 to 29.9) or obese (defined as having a body mass index of 30 or higher).[15]

In January 2000, Subway developed its best marketing pitch ever: college student Jared Fogel. Fogel once weighed 425 pounds. Determined to lose weight, he lived on a diet consisting of a Subway six-inch turkey sub for lunch and a twelve-inch Veggie Delite for dinner every day for almost a year. Subway built on Jared's story to heavily promote its "7 Under 6" line of low-fat, low-calorie sandwiches (seven six-inch subs, none with much more than three hundred calories and each with fewer than six grams of fat).

The move to introduce low fat and health as new dimensions of merit in fast food paid off handsomely for Subway. In 2000, the year Subway introduced its "Jared" campaign, the company's total sales growth was 47.5 percent, to $4.7 billion.[16] Although traditional fast-food chains still surpass Subway in dollar sales (McDonald's sales topped $40 billion worldwide in 2001, compared with Subway's $5.17 billion), Subway recently surpassed McDonald's in one key measure of success: As of December 2001, Subway reported that it had 13,247 shops in the United States, 148 more than McDonald's. And according to the quick-serve restaurant trade magazine *QSR*, Subway's per-store sales growth was about seven times the industry average for the year 2000. Subway's recent success coincides with— and is credited by some for contributing to—a new consciousness of the hazards of traditional fast-food fare and a push for more nutritious choices.

Not surprisingly, given public pressure and Subway's success, the other major fast-food chains have begun to offer health-conscious items of their own. Burger King recently introduced the 330-calorie Veggie Burger and has added reduced-fat mayonnaise to its menu. McDonald's has also introduced a couple of lower-fat options, including a Salad Shaker (with low-calorie, nonfat dressing) and a Fruit and Yogurt Parfait. Additionally, Wendy's offers healthful choices such as baked potatoes and chili and a new line of "Garden Sensations" salads.[17] The dangers of conventional fast food have also been the subject of considerable press attention, such as the recent popular movie *Supersize Me*.

As the Subway example suggests, creating a marketbuster in this category does not require massive new investment in wildly innovative solutions. It does require the imagination to envision how an existing package of needs and solutions might be subtly shifted. It helps, in addition, if the need you are targeting represents a large or growing issue. It helps even more if competitors are deeply wedded to serving the original set of needs, a practice that will tend to make their response to your move sluggish.

Prospecting Questions for Shifting the Dimension of Merit

Have you uncovered a new dimension of competing that is different from the current standard modes of competing?

Will it appeal to a large or growing segment of the market that is unimpressed with the current competitive criteria?

Are competitors largely wedded to the current criteria?

Has the very success of an existing solution created new problems that you might address?

Move #34: Create a Market via Cautious Evangelism

As shown in table 6-2, this move has the following pattern:

- An existing need

- A known solution

- Inadequate current solutions

Opportunities in this category are intriguing in that although a need or problem may be widely recognized, attempts to address it have proven inadequate. Perhaps the solution is too expensive, too complex, or too difficult to use. In any case, a new mass market will not emerge unless the market, technological, or cost barriers are cracked. What is often frustrating about such opportunities is that although the potential is often clear, insufficient utility has been created for customers to perceive existing solutions as valuable.

Example: What to Do with All Those Differing Digital Devices? The development of digital photography, PDAs, and speech recognition all fall into this category. The attraction of instant photos, electronic organizing, and devices that respond to voice rather than to keyboard input has long been recognized, but it took a long time for the relevant technologies to become cheap enough, usable enough, and good enough to attract a mass market following.

Example: A Failed Attempt—the CargoLifter. There are two ways *not* to tackle opportunities in this category: attempting to create the market entirely by yourself, or making a huge bet on your particular solution. The German company CargoLifter AG offers an example. Its founder, Carl von Gablenz, created the company in 1996 to pursue a concept of building blimps that could operate as "flying cranes." The idea was to overcome the inadequacy of alternative heavy cargo transportation approaches, such as the use of cargo airplanes. The heavy cargo market has long existed, but in the mid-1990s, as speed became important to many companies' competitive positions, firms began to seek ways of delivering heavy loads, such as military equipment, efficiently. Of particular interest were solutions for landlocked areas in which sea shipping was inadequate.

CargoLifter's airships were designed to hover 328 feet above the ground. Special loading frames would then lift the heavy materials into the blimp's cargo bay. To keep the airship from floating away when it was unloaded, special ballasts were designed that would be pumped full with 160 tons of water. CargoLifter's key differentiator (and the unmet need, given existing solutions) was that it required no runway. CargoLifter was envisioned to compete against Russia-based Volga-Dnepr Airlines, which had nine Antonov AN-124 aircraft that could carry 120 tons at speeds of 500 miles per hour. Boeing had its version, the BC-17, which could carry up to 80 tons of materials. This plane had been used mainly for military purposes, with plans to convert it to commercial uses. Both the BC-17 and the AN-124 required less runway space than typical commercial airlines but still required runways.

CargoLifter also promoted the ecological friendliness of the airship because it required energy only for propulsion and not takeoff and landing. It reduced road traffic and also had lower emissions than traditional forms of air transportation. One large blimp, the company envisioned, could also perform humanitarian aid by transporting enough food for 25,750 people for fourteen days.

CargoLifter's backers provided sufficient funds for the company to sink more than $250 million to develop an early version of the blimp. Unfortunately, the project was plagued by both technical and commercial problems. A trial run for an initial customer, Heavy Lift Canada, ended in disappointment when the blimp proved inadequate to the demands of a heavy storm. Other questions about its feasibility were raised, such as the willingness of customers to construct special sites for the blimp, the practicality of pumping so much water into an empty blimp (and emptying it again), and its slow speed and low-altitude flight. CargoLifter's bold attempt to create a new market for blimp-based heavy cargo hauling has now ended, at considerable cost to shareholders and the German government as well as development partners.

Prospecting Questions for Creating a Market via Cautious Evangelism

Have you uncovered a potential offering that will significantly attend to a problem that is not adequately addressed for a large emergent segment of the market?

Can you present your revised solution in a way that lets you thoroughly test market reaction before you commit major resources?

Are you convinced that this offering will be insulated from rapid matching by entrenched or emergent players?

The CargoLifter story reflects how difficult it can be to try to create a new market through the introduction of innovative solutions alone. In this category, we recommend that firms employ risk-reduction strategies (hence the caution with which we named this move). For example, you might identify a niche market for which the solution you can provide works well enough, and then migrate to the mass market as market and technical uncertainties ease. Another strategy is to mitigate downside risk through the use of alliances or partnerships with key customers.

The principle is that you can't tell whether something will work in reality when a need has not been adequately addressed before, so it makes sense to be somewhat cautious in your attempt to innovate.

Move #35: Build a Better Mousetrap

As shown in table 6-2, this move has the following pattern:

- An existing need

- A new solution

- An adequate current solution

This category of potential marketbusters has long caught the popular imagination. The idea here is that you think you can conceive of a better way of addressing a known marketplace need with a better offering, even though existing solutions are perceived as more or less adequate. The challenge you face is to make a sufficient difference to potential customers that they are willing to abandon previous solutions and switch to yours. A point to remember is that incremental, catch-up solutions are highly unlikely to provoke a switch.

Example: Attacking *TV Guide* with a Lookalike Offering. Giving insufficient thought to just how good or how different a new offering needs to be to get customers to change their behavior has often led to business failures. *TV–Cable Week* is a good example. The $55 million initiative was undertaken to launch a new television guide to listings, in direct competition to then-dominant *TV Guide*. Although a huge effort went into conceiving, designing, and writing the new magazine, it simply didn't provide enough value to persuade customers to switch. The initiative ended up being declared a significant flop for parent Time Life, Inc.

Example: Creation of a New Category: The Machine-Room-Free Elevator. In contrast, when the Kone Corporation of Finland introduced the first machine-room-free elevator in 1996, the key difference to building operators and contractors was immediately obvious. As its name suggests, elevators based on the Kone design can be constructed with the space and architectural constraints of a machine room to contain the equipment that makes the elevator run. This eliminates a significant source of cost as well as makes new building designs feasible. The Kone MonoSpace required less room, offered far greater design flexibility, and was also more ecologically friendly than its competitors. Launching the MonoSpace gave Kone a substantial advantage, in effect creating an entire market for machine-room-free elevators, which are growing in share of the new elevator construction business. It took competitors several years to catch up, by which time Kone had built a formidable position in the

---

Prospecting Questions for Building a Better Mousetrap

Have you identified an offering that is demonstrably superior on a dimension that is demonstrably attractive to an emergent segment of the market?

If the offering is not demonstrably attractive, can you deliver it at a lower price and still make good money?

---

mid-range elevator market in Europe, for which the MonoSpace is particularly well suited.

Success in this category of tectonic move is likely to go to the firm that offers a significantly better solution that also costs less. Growth comes from expansion of the established market as it converts from a previous solution, but more importantly from new markets for which previous solutions were too expensive or inaccessible. If you believe that the solution you've developed really does create an order-of-magnitude difference, then by all means launch aggressively to build first-mover position on solving an intractable problem in a new way.

Move #36: Undertake Inventive Missionary Work

As shown in table 6-2, this move has the following pattern:

- An existing need

- A new solution

- An inadequate current solution

The advantage of this category of opportunity is that you are not competing with something that has already been identified in the minds of possible customers as an adequate solution to the problem.

The disadvantage is that you must undertake the simultaneous creation of a complete solution and the education of a market, a task that increases uncertainty as well as the execution challenges that you are likely to face. This means that growth in this category is likely to be fairly slow. Dramatic growth won't happen until a major breakthrough in utility is recognized by a large market, and this doesn't usually occur until considerable experimentation has taken place in many smaller markets.

Example: The Turgid Pace of Voice Recognition Technology Adoption. The commercialization of voice recognition technology is an example of an innovation in this category. Although existing markets for this application can be readily identified, the technology itself is not yet good enough to offer a viable alternative to other solutions, such as data entry by keyboard. Nonetheless, voice applications are popping up in more and more places as the technology crosses the utility threshold for successive niche offerings. Voice commands are now found as replacements for telephone operators, in the Federal Express package pickup request system, and even in applications in mobile phones and in cars.

Example: Innovations in Health Care. There are many fascinating examples in health care in which new solutions have created considerable growth. Medical device manufacturer C. R. Bard, for instance, created a massive advantage for itself by introducing an innovative line of hernia repair products and ancillary services. By dramatically reducing the time and difficulty of having hernias repaired, Bard essentially created a new category of therapies in which it captured a dominant position. Considering that hernia repair is one of the most frequently performed surgeries, this marketbuster has allowed Bard to tap into a large and growing market (details are listed at http://www.crbard.com/news/viewNews. cfm?NewsID = 222).

With opportunities in this category, it makes sense to keep downside investments low and to preserve the option to discontinue investment if trials are unpromising.[18] Considerable experimentation

Prospecting Questions for Undertaking Inventive Missionary Work

Can you identify places in which large target segments are persistently unhappy with existing solutions? Have you got a potential solution that might work?

Will you be able to build a technically successful offering at limited cost and incrementally introduce it to clearly identified beta-friendly customers?

Can the process of market education and product development be unfolded without major initial resource commitments?

is likely to be involved, so it doesn't make sense to promise the boss or your shareholders that innovations here will provide dramatic new growth soon.

That being said, if this represents a market that you think will be highly significant for your future, you will want to develop early-warning indicators for market takeoff and prepare to move fast in the event that things seem to be coalescing around a particular solution.

Move #37: Make a Land Grab

As shown in table 6-2, this move has the following pattern:

- An emerging need

- A known solution

- An adequate current solution

Opportunities in this category make wonderful targets for established firms, because what is new is the need or problem to be addressed, but invention does not lie on the critical path to rapid market adoption. Typically, such opportunities arise because resources are made available that did not exist before or because long-term trends have allowed the emergence of a market segment that previously was either too small or too poor to be of much interest. Winning strategies often involve extending established competencies and capabilities to new opportunity spaces.

Example: Teaching America to Eat in Front of the TV. A fascinating example of a major success in this category of opportunity is the Swanson TV dinner. According to company lore, the dinner was created in the early 1950s, when inventor Gerald Thomas was attempting to come up with something to do with 520,000 pounds of leftover Thanksgiving turkey. The meat had not sold, and it was traversing the nation in refrigerated box cars because there was insufficient warehouse space for it.[19] Meanwhile, on an international plane flight, Thomas observed the flight crew testing metal trays for serving dinner to international passengers. He pioneered the concept of using a divided metal tray to separate various parts of the meal, solving one of the major objections to prepared precooked meals: that everything ended up as mush.

The TV dinner was introduced to the marketplace in 1954. For 98 cents, a customer got a full meal that included turkey, corn bread, gravy, buttered peas, and sweet potatoes. Along with the trend involving rapid commercialization of television, the Swanson dinners capitalized on the desire for convenience for two-earner families and on Americans' newfound fascination with home appliances. Nineteen million U.S. women took jobs outside the home during World War II and continued to work after the war ended, creating a new demand for food that required little time to prepare. In 1954, the first year of sales, Swanson sold more than 10 million dinners. Today, Americans consume 3 million Swanson dinners each week.

The TV dinner also influenced a number of secondary industries, including home freezers and microwave ovens. The name "TV dinner" was retired in 1962 to appeal to a broader audience. Today, one of the fastest-growing food segments worldwide consists of prepared, ready-to-eat, or nearly ready-to-eat foods.

Example: Selling to Sporting Women. Changing regulations often trigger the emergence of new needs. In the world of sports, Title IX legislation in the United States, which mandated equal access to funds for men's and women's sports, created many new markets for women's sports equipment and supplies.

Example: Changing Laws. Similarly, regulations can drive the emergence of new markets. Energy-efficiency requirements for automobiles, for example, have been a major driver for efforts by auto manufacturers to produce lighter cars that require less fuel—creating, among other things, the demand for substitute materials. Aluminum, for example, might be used in place of heavier steel. Recent bans of so-called white waste (disposable) products in China have created enormous demand for alternatives made from different materials.

Example: Helping People Quit Smoking. Another factor that can prompt the formation of a new market is a change in prevailing attitudes. For example, aggressive antismoking public relations campaigns and greater awareness of the health risks of smoking (not to mention bans on smoking in many public places) have created a new need for smoking cessation offerings. GlaxoSmithKline has capitalized on that new market with a product designed to help smokers quit. Nicorette gum is an alternative method of nicotine delivery, without the harmful tars that are prevalent in cigarettes. Nicorette is designed to slowly wean smokers from their addiction to nicotine, so that one day they will be dependent on neither cigarettes nor the nicotine delivered by the gum. Given the numbers that GlaxoSmithKline uses—46 million American smokers, 90 percent of whom want to quit and 70 percent of whom won't see their doctors—the market potential for an over-the-counter aid to quit smoking is enormous.[20]

Nicorette gum is sold in more than fifty countries and has gained scientific support. Several studies show that by using Nicorette, smokers are twice as likely to succeed compared with using willpower

---

Prospecting Questions for Making a Land Grab

As you evaluate the trends in your markets, are new needs emerging that you might have a solution to address?

Are there growing areas of persistent unhappiness or unease among your target segments?

Have segments become newly aware of social or other issues that might prompt a change in their behavior (such as certain industry categories falling out of favor, new health concerns, social changes with respect to acceptable behavior, and so on)?

Are you sure that your solution works for the target segment? Has it been validated by the market?

Do you know how to advertise, promote, distribute, and service the market? Do you need to do it yourself, or can you use existing infrastructure?

---

alone.[21] Since Nicorette became available as a nonprescription treatment, the number of adults attempting to quit smoking has significantly increased, to nearly 40 percent, according to a study of U.S. Census data presented on February 22, 2002, at the Eighth Annual Society for Research on Nicotine and Tobacco. This statistic adds to scientific evidence that providing over-the-counter treatment options for smokers increases quit attempts.[22]

Although there are no exact numbers available on the size of the stop-smoking market, the change in consumers' attitudes toward smoking indicates a huge potential for growth. In prescriptions, the market is valued at approximately $263 million. In 1998, sales of over-the-counter nicotine-replacement products exceeded $568 million, according to Information Resources, a Chicago-based marketing research firm. That's nearly double total sales in 1996, when these products first became available over the counter.[23] Nicorette is the sector's top global brand and is growing by 25 percent per year.[24]

Firms that win in this category genuinely have capabilities that address the emerging need, possess essential complementary capabilities (such as distribution), and are prepared to move aggressively.

Move #38: Create a Niche to Win

As shown in table 6-2, this move has the following pattern:

- An emerging need

- A known solution

- An inadequate current solution

Opportunities in this category can be highly profitable early attempts to address a whole new category of problems using existing capabilities. To the extent that your offering is better than alternatives (particularly better than nothing), you can create a substantial business as the market emerges and develops. The real risk of this kind of market is that better solutions are likely to emerge, because the problem that drives market growth has not yet been solved.

Example: Growing Through Increased Demand for At-Home Health Care. The growth of home health care product distributor Osim International was built on this form of tectonic customer shift. Osim's story began in 1980, when its chairman and chief executive officer, Ron Sim Chye Hock, set up a sole proprietorship in Singapore that sold kitchen appliances and household goods. Dr. Sim eventually diversified beyond household products to retail handheld massagers and blood pressure monitors. In expanding his product line to home health care products in the 1980s, Dr. Sim took advantage of an emerging set of customer needs focused loosely on taking care of oneself rather than going to a doctor or spending time in a spa to get a massage.

Busy lifestyles meant that time-pressed consumers were actively looking for alternatives to conventional approaches. Furthermore,

---

Prospecting Questions for Creating a Niche to Win

Can you identify small markets with new needs that are wealthy enough to afford to have the need met?

Have you developed something new in terms of products or services that might prove compelling to a customer group you have not served before?

Is the initial market large enough to minimize cash burn, or will you be able to capitalize on a large long-term market? If so, can you gain rapid dominance of the emerging market and lock out competitors?

Can you protect the long-term market well enough that you can build it without losing your profits to competitors?

---

people also showed that they were willing to do things themselves, thus eliminating waiting time and inconvenience. (Note that this trend also supports the success of other products and services, such as home test kits for diseases and developing family pictures.) Shifts in customer demographics and customer attitudes have also helped Osim's growth. Over the years, Osim's customer base has grown and changed. In the early 1980s, most of Osim's customers were in their late forties and early fifties, with many suffering from back or joint aches. Today, the bulk of Osim's clients are baby boomers aged thirty-five to fifty-five, for whom buying a blood pressure monitor or home sauna is a lifestyle rather than health decision.

Today, according to market research firms The Gallup Organization and ACNielsen, Osim International is one of the top brands of electronic health care products in Singapore and Hong Kong. Dr. Sim hopes to increase the number of outlets worldwide from 203 to 1,000 by 2008. In July 2000, Osim International launched its initial public offering and was listed on the main board of the Singapore Exchange. Since 1989, Osim has enjoyed strong growth every year.

In FY 1999, turnover rose 48 percent (to $103.1 million) and net profits tripled, from $2.3 million in 1998 to $7.7 million. In Q1 2002, Osim International posted 23 percent growth in profits (to $3.2 million) on a 22 percent higher turnover of $42 million. The company reported growth in all five of its key markets: Hong Kong, Singapore, Taiwan, China, and Malaysia.

In short, opportunities in this area can be considered a niche, at least at first. The key challenge is to gain penetration in the niche and then grow as the market grows.[25] Be aware, however, that as long as the solutions remain inadequate to the market's emerging needs, you will be vulnerable to someone else coming along with something even better than you can offer.

Move #39: Run the Arms Race

As shown in table 6-2, this move has the following pattern:

- An emerging need

- A new solution

- An adequate current solution

Opportunities in this category are among the most likely to inflict significant damage on those firms that pursue them. That's because many players are likely to perceive as attractive a substantial new need having a satisfactory solution, creating significant competitive entry and a likely eventual shakeout. In some cases, however, the solution you can provide is actually different from that offered by others and is protected by entry barriers, in which case this becomes a most attractive opportunity.

Example: Capitalizing on Rapid Growth in Demand for Wireless Internet Connections. This pattern is playing out in the market for gear that facilitates wireless networking in the home and workplace. An early winner has been Linksys, a company founded in 1988 and premised on the concept that cheap, usable networking (an emerging need) would offer significant opportunities. The Linksys offerings, targeted at home and small-business users, have been so successful that they dominate about 39 percent of the market for networking solutions by these users and have led to the acquisition of the company. Linksys has made *Inc.* magazine's list of fast-growing companies for five consecutive years, showing the power of addressing early needs with compelling solutions. Linksys was recently acquired for a healthy premium.

Example: The Rise (and Fall) of Discount Brokering in Germany. Far more common than Linksys's happy (at least so far) story are tales of firms entering attractive-looking markets, only to find that they are facing far stiffer competition than expected. Discount brokerages in European countries offer a cautionary example. As regulations began to permit discount brokers to operate, entrepreneurial firms such as Germany's ConSors entered with enthusiasm. Initial assumptions were that Germans, and other Europeans, would begin to trade with the same enthusiasm that Americans had, that the rising stock market would continue to provide incentives to trade, and (implicitly) that non-European firms were unlikely to enter with brokerage products. Initially, ConSors enjoyed dramatic growth, and its experience was widely reported in the media as a genuine Internet success story.

Unfortunately, as the new market proved to be attractive, others noticed, prompting massive numbers of new entries. In 1999 alone, sixty new players entered the market in Europe, and E*Trade, DLJDirect, Citi, and Schwab all announced intentions to expand in that region. Worse, the dramatic market reversals of 2000 depressed the appetite for trading, decreasing revenue from margin buying. ConSors ended up being acquired, and its parent company, Schmidtbank, found itself in bankruptcy (not entirely due to ConSors's fate).

So markets such as these are indeed wonderful opportunities, but the watchword is caution; you need to know how you will be insulated from competition, and you must be mindful of the many other players that are likely to be just as hungry as you are for the growth opportunities.

Prospecting Questions for Running the Arms Race

Are you confident that you can get a reliable solution in place quickly and profitably?

Are you being encouraged by the target segment to attend to this problem?

Are these customers willing to place advance orders—at good prices? Do you have a win-win?

Are they willing to take on beta models and learn with you?

Will you be able to protect your long-term position?

Move #40: Bet on Blue Sky Ventures

As shown in table 6-2, this move has the following pattern:

- An emerging need
- A new solution
- An inadequate current solution

Stop. Take a deep breath. Before moving any further with this category of opportunity, ask yourself the following questions:

- Are you prepared to wait three to five years or longer for this market to drive substantial growth?
- Do you have sufficient slack resources to sustain your efforts with respect to this market?
- Do you have management processes in place to appropriately recruit, compensate, reward, and respect people who are working on projects that are likely to be regarded by the rest of your firm as cash sinkholes?
- Are you prepared to tolerate many disappointments to learn what the business really is?

If you answered no to any of these questions, this type of opportunity may be very unattractive for you, at least in the near term. Don't say you weren't warned!

We have termed these kinds of opportunities *blue sky ventures* because they represent new-to-the-world problems, with new solutions that no one has yet figured out. In effect, you are dealing with problems people aren't sure they have, solutions that no one has yet experienced, in ways that may not even be technically feasible.

We're not saying that these kinds of opportunities aren't important. They are, because they can actually change the world and make a huge difference to your organization. We are saying that profiting from such opportunities is highly uncertain, and it will require considerable patience and adroitness from you as a manager. For these reasons, history suggests that success often goes to firms that are not incumbents in the affected industries.

Example: Pharmaceuticals, "Smart" Devices, and Clean Energy. A market that has the flavor of a blue sky venture includes new treatments for previously untreatable diseases, particularly those that stem from genetic problems affecting a subpopulation. Developing medications that are tailored to a specific genetic profile might be an example. Various forms of intelligent personal communication devices—such as "smart" clothing—probably also fall into this category. A host of innovations in the areas of clean, green energy, hydrogen-based batteries, and renewable fuels also fit this category.

Succeeding in ventures of this nature deserves far more comprehensive treatment than we can offer here. Fortunately, several excellent resources will point you in the right direction if you believe that you have an irresistible opportunity for the long term. To get started, see Block and MacMillan's *Corporate Venturing: Creating New Businesses within the Firm* and Leifer et al., *Radical Innovation: How Mature Companies Can Outsmart Upstarts.* Our previous book, *The Entrepreneurial Mindset,* also offers some useful tools for thinking about new-to-the-world types of businesses.[26]

Prospecting Questions for Betting on Blue Sky Ventures

Has no other approach recommended in this book shown you a less risky alternative, or are you so convinced of the enormous upside that you simply must go for this particular brass ring?

What evidence do you have of a huge upside, a controllable downside, and the sustainability of future profits?

The reality is that such businesses are apt to take a long period of sorting and experimenting to become genuine growth businesses. By imposing upon them the kinds of constraints and expectations that are appropriate for mature businesses, large organizations perennially mismanage these new ventures. They do, however, represent the most substantial risks for established organizations, which tend to dismiss or deny their potentially disruptive effects. Finding a new solution to a problem that was previously ignored is also a huge opportunity for entrepreneurs—pay no attention at your peril!

Action Steps for Exploiting Emerging Opportunities

Step 1: Audit your firm's orientation to the future by asking the following questions:

- Do you have a process for systematically pulling together information about the key trends and shifts that are likely to characterize your markets?

- Do you engage in future thinking, contingency analysis, scenario planning, or other ways of anticipating the future?

- Do you collect data that will help you see a trend in progress?

- Does your senior team spend enough time thinking about your own customer tectonics? Do people in your main functional areas also consider this topic?

- Are you alert to emerging needs and emerging sources of dissatisfaction in your key customer segments?

If the answers to these questions are no, it makes sense to begin to develop a better sense of the future. As a way to get started, we suggest something simple—perhaps allocating some time, say half a day each quarter, to think about future trends and get some input.

Step 2: Identify those trends that you believe may have an important influence on the needs of the customers you are already serving. What new needs might be emerging? What new solutions to existing needs might be emerging?

Step 3: Identify those trends that you believe may have an important influence on needs of customers you are *not* currently serving but that might prove important in the future, because they exist in markets that are adjacent to yours or because they may represent important growth opportunities.

Step 4: Speculate on how you might capitalize on the trends that you articulated in steps 2 and 3. What would make it worthwhile or crucial to take some action at this point? Do any of the trends represent a long-term risk to your business that suggests the need for immediate attention?

Step 5: Categorize the opportunity in terms of the moves shown in table 6-2. What does this tell you about your major challenges?

Step 6: Create a screening approach to determine which opportunities are worth further investigation. Then sort them into those you wish to pursue and those that you will leave for later.

Step 7: Establish a small working group or task force with the responsibility to flesh out the concept. (Be prepared to allocate resources to the members, and make sure that at least one of them is devoted full-time to exploring the possibilities.)

Step 8: For those markets that you consider to be most promising for your firm, begin to flesh out the resistance analysis table described in chapter 7.

Step 9: Decide how you might develop a project to pursue those opportunities you consider to be most important. Which of the following will you select?

- An innovation project driven from the senior level (as with the Apple Macintosh).

- A separate group with isolated resources dedicated entirely to the opportunity (the classic "skunkworks").

- A project folded into the ongoing work of a significant operating division. (Caution: This is likely to be successful only if the leadership of the division sees the market-creating activity as consistent with the current drivers of success for this group.)

Step 10: Initiate the project, bearing in mind the need for clarity of purpose (what defines success) and frequent stock-taking and testing of assumptions. Be prepared to stop or redirect the project should it appear to be heading off course.

7

EXECUTING MARKETBUSTING
STRATEGIES

I N THIS CHAPTER we graduate from the conceptual
task of identifying and designing a marketbusting move to the practical task of making it happen. We will describe a simple, effective
framework (developed mostly by Rita) for aligning key elements of
your strategy. Then we'll walk through a stakeholder analysis to
identify obstacles and barriers, explain our DRAT, or delay and resistance analysis table (developed mostly by Mac), and finish with a
short discussion of the political strategies you may need to consider
if you want to go after a marketbuster.

In chapter 8 we put it all together by sharing the story of how our
colleague Clive Mendes effected dramatic changes in the Italian au-
tomotive insurance industry as a new entrant, creating substantial
growth for its parent company, Royal & Sun Alliance, and substantial changes in the insurance market in Italy. The Royal Insurance
story illustrates the way many of our marketbusting lenses work
and gives an in-depth view of the implementation challenges of
making such an effort succeed.

How Ineffective Execution Can Derail Your Strategy

It's helpful to first get the issues of implementation firmly in your mind. Consider this: When you see a strategy that has been well executed, as opposed to one that has not, what makes the critical difference? When we ask this question of workshop participants, we usually get back a host of descriptors, such as "great leadership," "an excellent team," and "the right incentives." When we ask why good strategies derail, we get an equally long list, usually including things such as "unclear priorities," "wrong people in the wrong roles," and "poor leadership." Although there is nothing wrong with such lists, in our experience many of them are too vague to be actionable and they also omit one or more important elements.

Further, the things we tend to focus on when executing a strategy typically reflect our own interests and preferences. Some managers will emphasize structure, and they start (and, unfortunately, often finish!) their implementation efforts by moving boxes and lines on the organizational chart. Others get into rewards and incentives and spend the bulk of their time on the bonus program. Still others believe that a good budgeting process is at the heart of strategy, and they put their energy there.

The difficulty is that effective execution of a marketbusting strategy (or any other kind of strategy, for that matter) is an exercise in holistic alignment.[1] It is all about the concept of *and*. You need excellent leadership *and* clear direction *and* a sensible structure *and* the right people. A gap in any of these can and usually will dramatically impair the effectiveness of your implementation effort. The task at hand is thus to develop a way of comprehensively attending to everything it takes to execute the strategy.[2]

The Kite Model of Organizational Alignment

We use the metaphor of a kite to help you remember each element that needs to be considered and aligned. We like the metaphor for several reasons. First, it's simple, and we're big fans of keeping things simple. Although there is no shortage of models and frameworks for organizational alignment, we find many of them complex and hard to define. Second, no matter what you do to it, you can't *force* a kite to fly. You can cajole it or threaten it, even throw a hissy-fit, all to no avail. Your kite must be built properly and launched into the right context—just as your organization must be designed to execute and must be given a chance in a favorable context. Finally, for a kite to fly, each element of its construction must be assembled in the right balance. If you create a poor design, misalign things, or use inadequate materials, you won't get a kite. You'll get a disaster.

Following are the elements for organizational alignment that require attention:

- Agenda

- Norms and values

- News

- People structures and processes

- Allocations

- History

- Leadership behaviors

You can think of each element as creating an essential, integrated part of the kite you seek to build, as in figure 7-1. The plea here is that you think comprehensively and in an integrated way. Many managers have a pet device that they like to use, to the exclusion of the others. They focus on formal structure or the incentive system or the values of the organization and neglect the other forces they could be marshalling. This seldom works. You need to think about all of them, working together. Let's take each in turn.

FIGURE 7-1

Elements of Execution

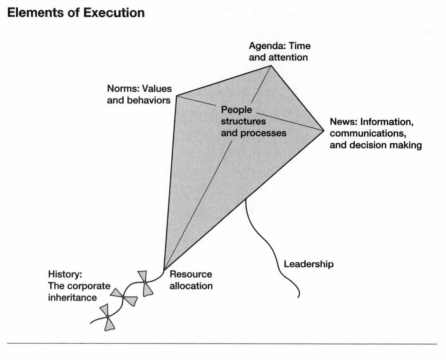

Agenda

Agenda refers, quite literally, to what you have on your agenda. What do you focus your time and attention on? This is not trivial. If you want to achieve a particular strategic outcome, you must put focus on it by making sure it is in the number 1, 2, or 3 spot on your agenda, and we mean all the time: at every management meeting you hold, on your calendar, in your conversation, and in the activities you pay attention to. When Rita wants to find out how sincere an organization is about what it says it wants to do, one thing she does is to audit the agendas of two or three recent management meetings. Let's say you tell us that you want to become more innovative. That's fine, but if matters related to innovation are in spot 18, right next to something like "material safety data sheet update," we can tell (and more importantly, so can the organization) that you don't really mean it.[3]

Setting your agenda to create focused attention on marketbusting should be your top priority. If you aren't paying that level of attention, neither will anyone else in the organization. Years ago, an insightful psychologist named G. A. Miller discovered that the number of things any human being can hold in short-term memory is about seven, plus or minus two.[4] This is the way human beings are programmed—and no amount of multitasking is going to change that reality. So, for your marketbuster to work, it had better be within that critical top seven.

Where do you start? Very practically. We suggest you begin with an audit. Collect some management meeting agendas—say, for the past three months. With a highlighter pen, mark the places where those issues you have decided are central to your strategy appear. Ask yourself: Am I giving those topics enough importance? Am I focusing management's attention where I think the future will be? Am I spending too much time on operational or urgent things and not enough on strategic issues that will be critical in the future?

Similarly, do a calendar audit. Review two or three weeks of how you are spending your time at work. Are you putting time into those things that are strategically important, or are you getting nibbled to death by dozens of meetings, e-mails, chance conversations, and seemingly urgent problems that pop up all day long? Now is the time to exert some control over that calendar—everyone who works for or with you will gauge what is really important to you by how you spend your time.

A final practice on the agenda question is consistency. Nothing breeds cynicism in an organization faster than leadership that is constantly changing what's on the agenda. We all know the syndrome. In January, we're all about innovation, and we launch a bunch of initiatives around new businesses. Come March, some bright spark has discovered enterprise resource management systems, and that spawns another series of work streams. By summer, it's implementing a balanced scorecard measurement system, and that brings on another slew of activities, and by fall, it's "What's up with the fourth quarter?" and the place is deluged with efficiency and productivity changes. No organization can effectively digest dozens of key strategic initiatives. Tough though it may be, a critical leadership task is to pick only a few—ideally, fewer than five—key priorities to focus on and stick to them.[5]

Norms

The *norms* element in our kite refers to the sets of explicit and implicit beliefs (often taken for granted) that guide day-to-day behavior in an organization. You can think of this as a company's "culture," although we tend to avoid that word because it tends to provoke a knee-jerk reaction from almost everybody. In executing a marketbuster, however, you need to give some thought to the norms that are in place in your organization.

Many kinds of value systems operate within organizations, and they can relate to performance in many ways.[6] If you want to create an organization that has the capacity to engage in marketbusting, however, there are some useful general principles to bear in mind.

First, marketbusting requires proactivity and risk taking. Therefore, your organization's norms must support and reinforce the advantages of intelligent risk taking. Some failure will occur and will have to be tolerated, or perhaps even celebrated, provided that it leads to vital learning.[7] Thus, you need to make sure that the distinction between intelligent failures and stupid ones is well understood and that the norms in your organization don't punish those who try and fail disproportionately to those who never fail because they never do anything. A nice example (reported by Sitkin) is a manager who in his personnel reviews insisted that his subordinates show him their "scrap heap" of things they had tried that didn't work out, as well as things they had tried that did.

Second, marketbusting, like any uncertain new strategy, requires an enormous amount of organizational learning. No matter how carefully you have thought things through, in reality life is never like your assumptions. This is when a critical human bias rears its ugly head. Called the *confirmation bias*, this concept refers to the human tendency to embrace information that confirms previously held assumptions and to ignore information that calls them into question.[8] Most of the time, we are well served by our confirmation bias, because it helps us separate meaning from noise; rather than have to pay attention to everything, we can focus on those few things that seem to be most important. In new and uncertain situations, however, it can be deadly, because people simply don't see important data that challenges their worldview.

Norms that reward challenging assumptions are therefore critical to the success of a marketbusting strategy. You want to avoid two cardinal sins: first, the sin of disagreeing with an observation or fact and saying nothing; and second, the sin of not actively participating in the debates that will reveal the correct information. So you'll need to reinforce questioning and criticizing behaviors—within the bounds of constructive learning and dialogue, of course.[9] Effective learning requires effective feedback, and that starts with people feeling that they have the obligation to bring facts to the table and make them explicit.

High-performing organizations also tend to have norms that stress personal accountability and follow-through, cause decisions to be made, and reward honesty.[10] Although it sounds obvious, these norms become doubly important when you are trying to accomplish something as demanding as a marketbuster, if only because without such norms you waste a whole lot of time on following up and checking on people.

News

By *news*, we mean the information-collection, meaning-creation, and communication processes at work in your organization. What, literally, is news in your company? And who are credible carriers of the message? In some companies, for example, no communication from headquarters is ever taken at face value; what you hear from your buddy down the hall represents the real scoop.

To start tackling the news issue, it's best to begin by looking at the measurements and indicators that you have in place. If you use something like Kaplan and Norton's Balanced Scorecard, what measures are on it? When were they last updated? Some companies are also aggressive in using a "dashboard"—a set of telling metrics kept constantly up to date, just like the indicators on an automobile dashboard. We then encourage you to identify which of your measures fall into the following categories.

Lagging: Lagging measures provide information about the consequences of past decisions and investments. Many corporate metrics are lagging—some because they are required by law or are useful for extrapolating trends. Last quarter's results, money in the bank, and in fact most financial measures are lagging.

Current: Current measures give information about the state of things at the moment. They are useful in helping you understand your current position and landscape. Factors such as current levels of employee or customer satisfaction, existing market share, and existing key ratios often fall into this category.

Leading: The hardest to quantify and the most important for purposes of marketbusting are the leading indicators. These are the often-fuzzy early warnings of what is to come. Unfortunately, it is here that many corporate measurement systems don't do their organizations justice; because they often are subjective and are open to interpretation, managers are often uncomfortable with leading indicators. Key uncertainties, trends, and looming issues fall into this category.

For marketbusting, leading indicators are critically important because they give you indications of whether you are heading in the right direction or are about to plunge over a cliff. To execute a marketbusting strategy, you must be explicit about the information you need, who needs to get it and when, and how you plan to interpret it. You also need to link those parts of the organization that need to work together to deliver it (for example, your technology groups and your marketing groups).

A good rule of thumb, as our colleague Willie Pietersen is fond of saying, is to remember that "what gets measured gets done." Thus, to execute your marketbuster you need to think about the key measures that will guide your organization to do the right thing. If you are in doubt about what kinds of things to measure, revisit the discussion in chapter 4 on the topic of key metrics in which we describe several kinds of measurement systems and show you how to develop or identify your own.[11]

Before you launch a marketbusting strategy, it is also vital that you know how you will get meaningful information. Unfortunately, as organizations evolve, their information systems often don't evolve as well, creating a disconnect between the information needs of the organization and what the information system can deliver. For some marketbusters, particularly those involving a change in your unit of business or a change in your key metrics, you will need to seriously consider (before you start, please!) whether the information you are currently collecting will provide the insights you'll need going forward.

Consider one of our clients, a maintenance-based business. Historically, the maintenance business was organized geographically, around customer locations. The client decided that shifting the customer definition—to reflect not location but ownership type—could be a marketbuster. Unfortunately, before the managers could even decide whether or not this made sense, they had six months' worth of data conversion to do. You probably guessed it—none of the company's historical records had been collected on the basis of customers; they were all based on physical location and geography! Had the company boldly launched the new strategy without taking the time to sort out their information needs, they could have found their implementation effort at a standstill, creating an opportunity for their competition to outflank them.

When you know what you want the news to be, the next challenge is to communicate it.[12] Ideally, you will plan your communications approach as carefully as you plan any other execution that is essential to launching your marketbuster. The first thing to remember is that you cannot overcommunicate. According to David Pottruck, for over twenty years the CEO of Charles Schwab and Company, he banks on having to do a lot of repetition. In fact, he suggests repeating the message seven hundred times before assuming that the organization has gotten it.[13]

Developing a communication plan involves the following steps:

1. Identify the audiences for your communication.

2. Identify the key outcomes you are seeking. Is the communication to inform, persuade, coordinate, appease, or what?

3. Identify the message that should go to each audience.

4. Identify the modes of communication you plan to use:

- One-on-one

- Group meeting

- Team meeting

- Organization's newspaper

- Project newsletter

- Letter

- Posters

- E-mail

- Web site

- Distribution of gifts

Note that the richer the message, the more likely it is that you will have to spend more time and be more personal than you would if you had a message that is easily transmitted. The simpler the message, the easier to repeat and lodge in people's heads.

5. Identify the communicator.

6. Identify the schedule on which communication will be done.

7. Determine how you will evaluate the effectiveness of your communication, and make adjustments as you go.

People Structures and Processes

It is with this element of alignment that many otherwise sensible managers impair their organization's ability to execute, because they get consumed by recasting formal reporting relationships. By focusing excessively on the formal structure and not on the other elements of the kite, they take care of what is often the easiest part of the alignment problem and fail to deal with what really needs to happen to orient people to a new set of tasks.[14] Effective leaders spend an enormous amount of time on people—selecting them, developing them, assigning them to tasks, and monitoring how they are doing. Bossidy and Charan (in their book *Execution*) and Christensen and Raynor (in *The Innovator's Solution*) have covered the territory of sensible people-management processes, so we won't repeat that material here.

What we would like to touch on are those considerations that might suggest to you that one or another structure makes sense for your marketbuster. First, will the new idea sustain the way you do business right now, or will it possibly cannibalize or weaken the existing business? The more it threatens the people in the existing business, the greater the value in locating the marketbuster team in a separate organizational structure. Why? The reason is that the people running your established businesses tend to have the wrong reflexes to run the new one, particularly if it's an entirely different kind of business (say, the core business is product-oriented and the new one is solutions-oriented). Further, existing businesses tend to have more organizational power behind them, leading them to undermine new businesses (even with good intentions).

However, do not fail to put in place mechanisms to settle disputes and make trade-offs between units that may overlap in customer contact or resource acquisition. You don't want internecine war, and you don't want to allow a nascent business that may not work out to inflict major damage, such as diluting your brand.

Finally, you should consider the incentives given to the people who are working on your marketbuster. One of your biggest difficulties will be to make sure that the rewards for trying, even without immediate success, are sufficiently attractive that people aren't punished for being put on the marketbuster team. One key practice is to make your incentives commensurate with the uncertainty facing the organization (see McGrath and MacMillan, *The Entrepreneurial Mindset*, for more on this idea).[15]

Resource Allocation

Say "budget process." The very term is enough to make some of us wince. And yet, managing the resource allocation process within your organization is perhaps the key mechanism through which you conduct strategies.[16] One major trap for many companies is substituting their budget and planning process for their strategic thinking process—but the two are not the same. Remember, first figure out your strategy, and then think about the planning and budgeting process that will make it happen.[17] One recent source reported that the typical billion-dollar company spent twenty-five thousand person-days assembling its budget every year![18]

A good rule of thumb is that when making allocations to new business opportunities, you need to give them disproportionate resources relative to their size. Thus, a fledgling business will need more intellectual power, more design skills, and more technology, proportionately, than a larger, established business. In many corporations, making sure that budgets are allocated to new businesses and that they don't find those resources siphoned away requires a champion to protect the resources at the executive level.

In designing your marketbusting strategy, it's essential to be realistic about how many and what kinds of resources you'll need, spread over what kind of time frame. Businesses don't evolve neatly year by year or quarter by quarter. Especially if you are launching an ambitious marketbuster, you may need to think in eighteen- to thirty-six-month stretches of resource commitment. A big mistake is to launch a marketbuster without making sure that you will have the resources necessary to follow up on the growth that hopefully will ensue. Often, that simply demonstrates a yummy opportunity to your competition, and there goes your marketbuster.

We are also intrigued by recent work being done on rethinking the typical corporate budgeting process. It may well be that your existing resource allocation process does not serve your organization particularly well, and a mini-marketbuster of your own may be to recapture some of the time and energy that go into budgeting and focus them on your offerings and markets.[19]

History

We include history under the topic of execution because in our experience it is a critical, often overlooked element. Like the tail of a kite, an organization's history can be enormously important for its stability. A kite with no tail lacks direction and balance. A kite whose tail is too big and heavy will never get off the ground.

As you are considering your marketbuster, think a little about your organization's history. Which elements do you think have value and need to be preserved? Which elements could use a change? Over time, any organization collects practices and people that no longer serve it well. When thinking about a marketbuster, you may want to think about changes to that history as well.

Leadership

Finally, like the string of a kite, your organization's leadership directs and guides your organization. So many volumes have been written about leadership that we will confine our comments here to a few key practices we have observed that are essential to executing a marketbusting strategy.

First, have you specified what the success of the strategy will be and therefore what the key priorities for the organization are? If people are not clear on their goal and focus, it's almost impossible for them to execute effectively.

Second, have you thought through where you personally will need to intervene to clear paths for your people? There are times when senior leaders need to get involved, whether to break a stalemate within the company, to persuade a doubting potential customer, or to soothe ruffled feathers among collaborators. If the right interventions don't get made, projects can bog down and precious time can be lost.

Third, have you done everything you can to create the commitment to executing the marketbuster? This question covers obvious things such as your agenda and allocation of resources as well as subtle things such as the symbolic content of what you do.[20] Leaders often forget that everything they say and every move they make are subject to interpretation and are given meaning by the people watching them. Do your symbols and sound bites match your aspirations? If they don't, you've got trouble.

Fourth, have you employed different management styles for different levels of uncertainty? Highly certain businesses can be managed fairly conventionally. For uncertain ones, different rules apply. This is where unconventional practices—failing intelligently, being "roughly right," and being parsimonious until assumptions are validated—all come together.

Finally, are you personally managing the process of redirecting or even shutting down projects well? This includes distinguishing bad luck from bad management, avoiding escalation of commitment, and having the discipline to stop investment in a strategy that is not making progress. These activities are among the least fun parts of a leader's job, but they are critical. If you don't have the ability to stop things, your resources can become tied up in suboptimal projects, leaving the really good ones starved for growth options.

Insightful Anticipation of Obstacles and Barriers

Making a marketbusting move isn't easy, or others would already have done it. Further, your success usually comes at someone else's expense. So it's vital to think through the obstacles as thoroughly as you can before you get out there and get whipsawed by fate.

Obstacles and barriers to your potential marketbuster fall into two major categories. The first are external factors. Second are internal factors, which comprise sources of potential resistance from within your firm or stem from a lack of needed capabilities. To deliver your marketbuster to the customer set, you may have to identify and build one or more entirely new capability platforms.

Table 7-1 illustrates the delay and resistance analysis table (DRAT). The DRAT table is a shorthand way of identifying those forces that might get in your way.

TABLE 7-1

DRAT (Delay and Resistance Analysis Table)

Source	Description
External	
Powerful incumbents	Adversely affected players external to your firm can make your life miserable if your move is not in their interests.
	Example: Sun Interbrew, attempting to sell beer in Russia, experienced expected opposition from vodka manufacturers, but also from organized crime and even challenges from the Russian tax authorities, who required cumbersome documentation.
Opposition from advocacy groups	Sometimes a marketbuster will trigger an adverse reaction from an advocacy group that could make your move an issue and impede or torpedo your attempt.
	Example: Procter & Gamble found itself facing a firestorm of criticism upon introducing the Olestra fat substitute in 1996. The criticism stalled the growth of a hoped-for $1 billion product.
Risk to key external stakeholders	If your success creates actual or perceived risk for customers, suppliers, your channels, or your alliance partners, they may resist your efforts unless you can ameliorate the risk.
	Example: Until a reference order from a reputable firm could be shown, an oil refinery customer in Africa resisted purchasing a new filter cloth material.
Inertia	Change is hard work: Unless you have a compelling reason that things should be done differently, external stakeholders are likely to prefer the status quo.
	Example: Although new technologies such as smart cards were heralded, their advantages to customers have simply not been sufficient to overcome the inertia of existing ways to pay bills.
Disruption of customer's system or process	If your marketbusting move requires your customers to change expensive embedded systems or long-established practices, they may be inclined to resist no matter how intriguing the upside.
	Example: Until German software manufacturer SAP figured out a process for systematizing the installation of its enterprise software, customers were reluctant to undergo the traumatic process changes that such installation often required.
Changes in standards or regulations required	Governments and regulatory bodies are not known for their fleetness and adaptability. If a change of this kind is on your critical path, you may face a long, hard slog.
	Example: Replay TV and TiVo devices allow consumers to skip commercials and promote video file sharing. These innovations were instantly met with lawsuits from TV networks and copyright infringement claims by content providers.

TABLE 7-1 *(continued)*

DRAT (Delay and Resistance Analysis Table)

Source	Description
Internal	
Internal political maneuvering	Individuals such as those in charge of today's business may feel politically threatened by your success.
	Example: IBM created an alliance called Integrion with 17 banks, intending to provide total back-office support processing for all of them. The venture dissolved in 2000 because it turned out that this level of outsourcing was more than the people within the banks had counted on supporting.
Reluctance or resistance by those needed for active implementation	Individuals whose active involvement is needed for implementation may resist.
	Example: A bank whose marketbuster involved global operations continued to reward people for local performance—with the result that nobody did anything on the global initiative, and it failed.
Resource constraints	You may experience shortfalls in key resources needed to implement.
	Example: Sonera, the telephone operating company in Finland, tried to bust the market by moving into advanced services but found itself strapped for funds after the collapse of the telecom bubble and had to pull back on its strategy.
Platform changes required	Disconnects between your current capability platforms and any of the following new platforms needed to render your marketbuster deliverable
Human resource and skills platforms	Royal Insurance Italy had to develop completely new skills in order to deliver direct line insurance, ranging from online systems design and delivery to risk analysis and management capabilities.
Logistics platforms	Amazon.com had to create an entirely new logistics system for delivery of books ordered by online customers.
Distributor platforms	Merrill Lynch had to accommodate an entire brokerage network when it opened its discount brokerage business
IT and database platforms	Logistics.com had to develop all the database and data-mining programming needed to facilitate trucking contracting.
Technology platforms	ARM is constantly challenged by the need to incorporate the latest RISC technology in its chips, but current users of old chips are reluctant to switch to the new chips until there is sufficient evidence of long-term reliability.
Assets, operations, and systems platforms	Air Products and Chemicals needed to develop and install large numbers of gas separator systems with associated maintenance and service networks to implement its on-demand industrial gas delivery strategy.

Developing Your Own DRAT Table

As part of your execution challenge, you need to think through which types of resistance you can expect to encounter, and then develop countermeasures. One way to get started is to use the list in table 7-1 and fill in your marketbusting team's assessment of your situation. Chapter 8 provides an illustration of the DRAT table for the Royal Insurance Italy example.

Tactics for Accelerating Implementation

In thinking about how to overcome some of your DRAT table obstacles, you might consider some techniques we have seen companies use.

Identify and mobilize allies. Identify the parties inside and outside the firm who stand to benefit from the success of your marketbuster. How might you mobilize them to overcome some of the sources of resistance? What can you offer them to help you?

Find lead steers. Analyze the target customer base to see whether you can identify customers who are highly respected, opinion-leading potential lead steers—people whose support of your move will provoke others to follow. Develop a specific strategy to entice these lead steers to play the role.

Underwrite risks for early supporters. Think about the key risks that the first supporters of your marketbusting move will be taking, and see whether you can develop a strategy to underwrite that risk for them.

Run in parallel. To the extent possible, run your current operation in parallel with the marketbusting move so that you can maintain reliability and quality while you debug and develop proficiency with the marketbuster system.

Pilot with a beta customer. Look for a customer that is excited by the potential first-mover benefits and is willing to suffer the risk and inconvenience of being a special beta customer. Beware, though, of alienating other customers.

Conduct self-inflicted testing. If it is possible, use a "customer" inside your firm, especially in your own department, to test your marketbuster. Then all your development and debugging effort will be invisible to the competition and will not be felt by key stakeholders.

Action Steps for Executing MarketBuster Strategies

You and your team should work your way through several processes. In the following list we offer detailed descriptions of what to think about, especially for the kite analyses. Be careful not to get bogged down in these steps. Focus only on the key components of each one. Chapter 8 illustrates this process.

Step 1: If you have not yet done so, fill out your version of the DRAT table.

Step 2: Work through your DRAT table and identify specific obstacles (people, departments, outside organizations) that will delay or obstruct your moving from the current system to the future system. Review the tactics listed earlier for accelerating implementation to see whether you can apply them to your marketbuster.

Step 3: Describe each element of the kite in the business as it is being run today. Specify the main features and drivers of agenda, norms, and so on.

Step 4: Envision and describe what the main drivers of each element of the business system will look like when the marketbuster is in place and running successfully in the future.

- **Agenda.** Decide which key activities will require the attention of the team and which current activities will receive less attention. Reach agreement on which members will spend how much of their time on which major activities. Be specific. After the marketbuster program is under way, perform regular agenda audits. Review the past month's worth of management meeting agendas and the past two to four weeks of your calendar. Does your agenda reflect your marketbusting goals? If it doesn't, redirect it. Market-busters should be number 1, 2, or 3 on every management meeting list and should occupy at least 20 percent of your own personal calendar time. If you mean it, live it.

- **Norms.** Analyze your norms. What principles should drive decision making? Does everyone understand and agree? What key behaviors are desirable as the marketbuster moves forward? Does everyone understand and agree? What behaviors will be sanctioned? Are honest feedback and debate valued? Are people open to having their assumptions challenged? In particular, do you need to do some work to recognize the importance of intelligent failures?

- **News.** What measures are used to monitor successful progress? Do you have a measurement system that lets you monitor the progress of your marketbuster? Do you have enough leading indicators in your system? What information are you focusing on? Are the team members aware of the information needs of others, including timeliness and quality? Are team members confident that they can get enough information to take action?

- **Allocations.** Analyze your resource allocation process. Are sufficient resources (funds and talent) available for your marketbuster? Are they protected from looting by the core business? Are team members able to secure more resources if needed? Is there a process for this? Is the reward system designed to reward appropriate performance—that is, are the right people eligible for appropriate formal and informal rewards? Do you have the right authority structure for people to be rewarded with the right timeliness? Are the reward processes visible enough? Do you have a similarly well-defined sanction structure?

- **Structure.** Think about your formal and informal people structure. Is there clarity about which individuals or sub-groups have decision-making authority and who has responsibility for key outcomes? Are decisions made at the right level—can decisions be made fast enough? Are reporting and working relationships clear? Are the right people working together? Do you have a system for getting the right people in the right jobs? Do all those in the program have the confidence that they and others have the competence to carry out their tasks?

- **History.** What traditional ways of doing things will you keep because they add value, and what will you need to change? Evaluate new routines, planning processes, monitoring and control processes, and budgeting and resource allocation processes.

- **Symbols.** What powerful, symbolic behaviors, processes, and icons are respected? Which will you keep, and which will you change? What ceremonial events, communications, celebrations, recognition, and logos can be put in place to reinforce your marketbuster? Also assess your own leadership and communication behaviors. How can you elevate your level of activity in defining success, clearing paths, creating commitment, creating climate, and managing disappointment?

Step 5: Identify the specific changes that are needed for each element of the kite to move the existing business system to its future form.

Step 6: Decide what major challenges you will need to meet in removing obstacles to reconfiguring the kite.

Step 7: Identify champions who will be responsible for accomplishing the changes and removing obstructions. Define closure (how you will determine when the change has been accomplished) and key progress milestones.

Step 8: Define the early actions and next steps for each element in this new system so that this alignment is achieved and the DRAT obstacles overcome. Have your champions develop action steps and the milestones where they will assess progress.

Step 9: The more uncertain the outcome of a marketbusting move, the more important it is that you develop a discovery-driven plan (DDP) that allows you to convert your assumptions into knowledge before investments are made. The DDP methodology is covered in detail in our first book and a *Harvard Business Review* article, so we will not cover the details here.[21]

If this looks like a lot of work, that's because it *is* a lot of work. But we find that it is work well worth doing, especially if you don't waste time getting tangled in the little issues but instead focus on main issues and major obstacles. Marketbusting is difficult enough if you have paid attention to alignment and obstacles. It can be horrendous if you have not.

8

MARKETBUSTER CASE STUDY

ROYAL INSURANCE ITALY

IN 1994 Clive Mendes carried out a strategic review for Lloyd Italia Spa, which was at the time the largest Italian subsidiary of the British Royal Insurance Group. At the time, the Italian legislative and cultural framework was undergoing many changes, and Mendes believed that an opportunity was developing to bust the market for personal lines insurance, particularly motor (auto) insurance.

When Mendes looked at the auto insurance market, he saw a large market (30 million vehicles). Some three hundred insurance companies were offering coverage, but three large, well-known Italian "institutions" dominated: SAI, RAS, and Generali.

Distribution was predominantly by means of tied agents—self-employed agents who worked exclusively for one company. Even a medium-sized company could have several thousand of these agents, whose work arrangements varied from one-man shows to sizable organizations involving a number of subagents. This scenario is not very different from that in many European countries, with two exceptions. First, auto insurance premiums and policy conditions were set by the Italian government and, second, there was an extra-ordinary degree of customer dissatisfaction with the insurance service received.

Mendes knew that the European Union was about to require all European governments to "liberalize" their auto insurance markets. This would mean that individual companies would be free to set their own prices and conditions. He guessed that most Italian companies would not be ready, after many years of simply administering a government tariff, to make a rapid transition to a more advanced, personalized form of pricing. Mendes's view was that in many cases they lacked the knowledge, the data, and the necessary in-depth statistical analyses. What's more, there was an inherent cultural conservatism or mindset that would make it difficult for most insurers to make the needed radical changes in the short term. They would get there eventually, but in the meantime there would be a few years for a creative first-mover to bust the market and redraw the playing field.

What Mendes had in mind was creating a direct distribution company somewhat similar to Direct Line in the U.K. Direct Line was the first U.K. company to take advantage of advances in IT and in call center technology to sell auto insurance to customers over the phone as well as manage customer claims and damage repair from centralized locations. This model relies on operating efficiency to create price advantages as well as improved customer service from longer operating hours and homogenous, controlled interaction with clients. The Royal Insurance Group had also adopted this model in the U.K., setting up a direct company in 1988 called The Insurance Service (TIS) and, around the same time, a small but very successful company in Barcelona called Regal Insurance Club.

TIS operated very similarly to Direct Line. It had a fairly wide target group of customers and was focused on operating excellence as its principal strategic positioning. Regal was different. It had a narrower target market—the best drivers—and, as its name suggests, customers who qualified (for the club) with a good driving record were rewarded with excellent service and attractive prices.

Royal Insurance, however, was not simply a clone of Direct Line, nor of TIS and Regal. Royal Insurance had to succeed in a very different market. Mendes believed that it was possible to put together a recipe that would take advantage of a uniquely differentiated approach focused on the high degree of customer dissatisfaction with auto insurance in Italy. Customer research suggested that customers considered the purchase of compulsory third-party auto insurance as something akin to a tax. They strongly resented buying it, and often the experience was unpleasant and frustrating from a customer perspective. Claims were processed slowly by big, bureaucratic institutions, and customers had no voice or means of reaching decision makers except through the agents, who often didn't have the influence they professed to have. Importantly, customers also generally tarred all insurers with the same brush. In short, insurance was a grudge purchase.

Therefore, Mendes decided that he could be successful only if the business system created happy customers who would spread the news that there was a different type of insurance company in the market—one that sold the kind of products that customers wanted to buy, at prices that were reasonable, and with a quality of service that was second to none. He also believed that if he was successful and consistent in pleasantly surprising his customers, then, in addition to spreading the word to family and friends, they would be more loyal, or at least their inherent conservatism would make them less likely to be tempted by competitors' offers.

Thus there was a major opportunity to revolutionize the attribute map at several links in the consumption chain in the following ways:

- By reducing several dissatisfiers: purchasing, claims processing, and customer service

- By adding positive differentiators in the form of lower premiums for drivers having good risk profiles

- By offering a menu of coverage from which to choose

The challenge therefore was to design a company that would stand out from the rest by outperforming its rivals in customer satisfaction and profitability.

Business Philosophy

The Royal Insurance Italy business was founded on the following five basic principles, which Mendes and his team view as the keys to long-term success.

Customer Satisfaction. This belief is ingrained in the company's psyche. All processes, products, and activities are built from the customers' perspective and incorporate their views and priorities. The company obtains this information directly from customers by means of feedback processes such as questionnaires, focus groups, a "customer charter" (discussed in a moment), and an attention to customer relations throughout the organization. This has resulted in delivery of prize-winning customer satisfaction and consistently high customer-retention levels of more than 90 percent.

Operational Excellence. Similarly, Mendes believed that he could sustain his initial success by pursuing levels of operational efficiency that were better than the norm. Operational excellence means getting things right the first time and getting things done as quickly as possible at the lowest required level of competence in the organization and with maximum automation. Over the years the firm has redesigned the way it does things. Wherever possible, the preference is to make step changes in quality rather than incremental improvement.

Personal Responsibility. Royal employs people who enjoy taking responsibility for doing a good job and for developing themselves and others while being passionate about providing solutions to customers' needs. Royal's leaders (formal and otherwise) set the example to support this ideal, and the rewards and recognition systems have been recast to ensure that successes are recorded, rewarded, and celebrated. With the exception of a few technical positions and some outstanding people, the company's preference is to choose managers and staff from outside the insurance industry.

Image Management. Royal Italy was aware of the importance of its brand as an instrument for influencing its key constituents: customers, distributors, staff, and society. It has kept careful control of its image and has actively used every medium to ensure the consistency of its message, including advertising, promotions, public relations, public affairs, and customer relations management. The name Royal Insurance was chosen because customer tests showed that it had positive connotations of service, quality, and tradition—attributes that the company thought it would need to convince customers of its seriousness as well as to develop its own institutional image power to match that of the large Italian insurers.

"Knowing Our Business." The business philosophy of Royal Insurance is supported by a highly sophisticated data management system that covers everything from technical knowledge to understanding customers as well as understanding and influencing the market environment.

Making a MarketBusting Move

Capitalizing on the opportunity to bust the market via exploitation of a shift in industry dynamics, Mendes and his team put together a six-pronged marketbusting program to capitalize on the regulatory changes by the Italian government:

1. Radical resegmentation at the purchase link

2. Radical changes in the service link

3. Revolutionized pricing

4. Radical new distribution links

5. A radical attack on the awareness link of the consumption chain

6. A major attack on key metrics

Radical Resegmentation at the Purchase Link

Royal Insurance radically resegmented the market to capture a prime target market of private car drivers who are over thirty-five, have a proven good driving record, and drive cars for social or commuting purposes. Royal Insurance did not cover commercial vehicles or fleets.

With this target market in mind, Mendes and his team assembled products that have the following compelling attributes.

Personalized and modular products: The customer chooses the desired coverage, limits, and so on. Products are simple but offer wide coverage with no hidden clauses or compulsory deductibles. Unlike rival offers, which tend to be "standard products," coverage is modular, and customers can tailor policies to their own needs.

To quote Mendes, "Customers are smart and rational in their choices but emotional in their affiliations, and if you involve them they will become your allies and your champions."

Transparent products: Royal Insurance policies were the first in Italy to be written in plain Italian, doing away with complex, legal language.

Meritocracy: Prices vary so that good drivers pay less than those who are not so careful.

Radical Changes in the Service Link

Royal Insurance became the only insurance company in Italy and the first in Europe to offer its customers a customer charter ("Carta dei Diritti"), which contains a written promise of the service standards customers can expect. The standards, which relate to access to services, claims performance, and privacy, are extremely challenging. For example, the company promises inspection of accident damage within forty-eight hours, payment of refunds within three working days, and payments of claims within seven days.

This innovative written promise was introduced to underline the company's commitment to customers in the form of guaranteed service standards but also served to focus internal attention on the key quality and efficiency indicators. Furthermore, it serves as a rallying point for staff, who take pride in the unrivaled quality of their work.

The seriousness of the "Carta dei Diritti" is demonstrated by a financial penalty that is paid to a customer as an apology when the promised standards of service are not delivered. Royal Insurance's performance in maintaining service standards is audited annually by a group comprising Price Waterhouse Coopers and randomly selected customers, who have access to any information they ask for. This is an important formal and symbolically powerful moment of interaction with customer representatives. It also helps keep the service standards relevant to customers, maintains internal company performance at the most efficient level, and makes it difficult for competitors to imitate the Royal Insurance approach. In the spirit of transparency, the results of the audit are published in the major national newspapers, and a copy is mailed to each customer.

Revolutionized Pricing

Royal Insurance introduced a number of revolutionary pricing policies.

Personalized meritocratic prices: By asking a series of questions about a customer's lifestyle and driving style, the company can statistically estimate his or her propensity to have an accident. There are several million possible price combinations, meaning that prices can be accurately correlated to each customer. Each driver pays more or less depending on his or her risk profile.

Pricing innovations: An innovative "no claims discount" enables good drivers to reach the lowest price after only five years instead of the fourteen years of claims-free driving offered by most other companies.

Segmentation and selectivity: At the heart of the business is a state-of-the-art executive information system, based on SAS technology, that lets the company easily and quickly monitor the performance of the portfolio. Royal Insurance can forecast accurately and intervene rapidly to take advantage of positive market developments as well as take any needed corrective action in a timely manner. The company can change prices in a matter of a few hours.

Radical New Distribution Links

Royal Insurance added radically new distribution links.

Call center: Royal Insurance was one of the first insurance companies in Italy to distribute its products by call center. The call center, which employs about three hundred fifty (FTE) people, has been the source of about 68 percent of the firm's business to date. The call center is the only one in Italy to be open seven days per week with extended operating hours. Staff members work in shifts to service business needs.

Internet: Mendes realized that the Internet would be a powerful new distribution channel, and so Royal Insurance has had a Web presence since 1996. It has developed the Internet site over the years and has been actively selling on the Web using an automatic process since 1999. Currently 40 percent of new business comes from this source, and the proportion is growing, with obvious cost-saving advantages and greater satisfaction for customers. Royal Insurance is a recognized industry leader in e-business.

Partner system: In 1998, Royal Insurance developed an extranet (called Partner System) that is used to service business partners. Partnerships are not core to Royal's business, but this B2B tool has enabled it to gain additional business from nontraditional partners that have been attracted to Royal by its reputation for quality. These partners include several banks, a supermarket chain, and car manufacturers.

A Radical Attack on the Awareness Link

Royal Insurance speaks directly to its customers through various advertising media (print, television, posters, the Internet, and so on). It overtly employs a message of trust in its customers and emphasizes the "intellectual equality" of the contracting parties; in other words, customers are mature and are capable of choosing according to their needs.

Frequent communications are also a feature of Royal Insurance's customer relations system. In addition to an annual letter reminding customers of the need to renew their policies—an approach typical of relationships with most insurance companies—Royal Insurance uses many other opportunities, such as birthdays, to communicate with customers. So when renewal time comes around, Royal is fresh in the customer's mind. The style of the communication is novel and sophisticated, and as exciting as it is possible to be with an insurance product.

As we mentioned earlier, in the spirit of transparency the results of the Price Waterhouse Cooper audit are published in the major national newspapers and a copy is mailed to each customer. In this way, Royal Insurance has been successful in establishing a brand image of both innovation and traditional seriousness, together with a reputation for customer focus.

A Major Attack on Key Metrics

Many people think that the source of advantage in direct insurance is a lower-cost administrative structure. As a result, the basic business model Mendes developed is not necessarily obvious.

The technical business proposition is as follows: By controlling the quality of driver insured—and therefore excluding from the portfolio drivers who are statistically more likely to have accidents—Royal Insurance can offer good drivers high-quality service at a lower price than they would pay elsewhere, while still receiving from these drivers a higher contribution to its profit. (In rough terms, the usual 20/80 rule applies: Some 20 percent of people cause 80 percent of accidents.) Royal Insurance applies the basic principle that each customer pays for the risk that he or she represents.

The company manages the quality of its portfolio principally by means of a performance management system developed in-house.

This system provides management information, advanced statistical analysis, decision support, planning and forecasting, and customer relationship management (CRM) functionality. This state-of-the-art system gives Royal Insurance important competitive advantages in pricing, portfolio management, and market positioning.

This combination of good price and high-quality service creates a "virtuous spiral" effect, with fast growth and high retention levels repaying the initial investment in a relatively short time. The result is that it was possible to create an important, profitable, low-cost-base personal lines insurer in the space of a few years. The direct relationship and the intimate knowledge of the customer base enable cross-selling and up-selling from this platform and permit various kinds of future vertical or horizontal integration.

In combination, the strategies lead to a powerful key metrics business model that not only generates passionately loyal policyholder revenue but also reduces key cost metrics in the following ways:

Correct risk selection	Reduces technical costs
Operating excellence	Reduces operating costs
Information access and management	Reduces operating costs
Culture of empowerment	Reduces operating costs
Image management	Reduces acquisition costs
Outstanding service	Reduces retention costs

From the perspective of the customer and staff member, the system is simple and straightforward, even if data-processing and data-mining complexities lurk behind the scenes. It is this data technology that renders the business simple. Royal Insurance built scalable call center, claims-handling, and Internet environments to service the processes required by the relatively simple Royal Insurance formula.

Results

The results were, as expected, low growth in the initial years as the new concept established itself. This was followed by ever-increasing customer acceptance, retention in the range of 90 percent, declining costs, and an exceptionally high quality portfolio: nonvolatile loss ratios in the low 80 percent range in what is considered a difficult market, with an average compulsory-motor-loss ratio (a measure of costs) in excess of 110 percent.

The original plan was to build a portfolio of 100,000 policies by the end of 2001; the actual result was 250,000 by that point, and about 280,000 customers by the end of August 2002, of whom about one-quarter were recruited from the Internet. This placed Royal Insurance in a leading position in the direct market and prepared it well to continue its rapid growth. At launch the company employed forty-five persons, a number that has grown to five hundred at the company's headquarters in Milan.

Royal Insurance is a two-time winner of the Databank BICSI award for customer satisfaction and is the recognized industry leader in this area. It was also awarded the first Databank prize for excellence in e-business in February 2002.

The success of Royal Insurance has had an important effect on how auto insurance is transacted in Italy. A number of local and foreign companies entered the direct market, such as Linear (Gruppo Unipol, based in Italy); Lloyd 1885; RAS (based in Germany and Italy); and Allstate (from the United States). In addition, the direct and traditional markets have reacted by making changes to pricing structures, moving to personalized tariffs (in which prices for insurance vary by individual), and modifying no-claims discount mechanisms.

Overall, the insurance market has become aware of the importance of retaining valuable customers and the need for satisfying customers. Some traditional companies (such as AXA, based in France) began using call centers and direct techniques to service their agency networks. Others, such as Italy's Cattolica, have reorganized their claims-handling structures to mimic those of Royal Insurance.

Several companies have introduced customer charters or published service standards. The Italian legislature (which initially found it difficult to accept some of the Royal Insurance innovations) has passed laws that embody concepts, such as the "risk profile," that Royal Insurance introduced into the market.

Thus we see that a truly successful marketbuster will inevitably provoke a competitive response, and the continued success of Royal Insurance will depend, as in many other cases in this book, on the capacity of Royal's new parent company *not* to rest on its laurels but instead to either continuously and entrepreneurially innovate (as we suggest in our first book) or to begin looking for a follow-on marketbuster.

Table 8-1 outlines the threats faced by Mendes when he began the company.

As you can see, Mendes was facing a formidable task. In a way, this is why no one else in the industry was mobilizing for change and why, after he overcame these forces, he could expect his marketbusting move to run for some time. Table 8-2 shows the forces Mendes was able to marshal.

In addition to the DRAT table, we look at Mendes's kite challenges in table 8-3.

Because Mendes was creating an entirely new organization, he really didn't have an existing kite to work with, and that gave him considerable latitude to create an organization that could uniquely deliver this strategy. Normally, we would encourage you to start from where you are, think about where you need to go, and specify the gaps so that they become extremely operational for you and your team. This approach should show you how, by focusing on the essentials and avoiding unnecessary details, you can provide the selected champions with an integrated kite that frames the challenges they need to overcome to develop a plan having all the requisite details. In the example in table 8-3, notice that each cell of the table has three to six core drivers that integrate action across the entire kite.

TABLE 8-1

DRAT Table, Royal Insurance

Source	Which of these can you anticipate? Be specific: Which people, departments, firms will be a source of resistance?
External	
Powerful incumbents	Major insurers: SAI, RAS, Generali
Opposition from advocacy groups	Pressure from incumbents on Italian insurance regulators
Risk to key external stakeholders	Unwillingness of tied agents to risk wrath of major insurers, unwillingness to change current comfortable bureaucratic and indifferent processing of sales, claims
Inertia	Worse than inertia—antipathy of insureds
Disruption of customer's system or process	Unwillingness of potential customers to go through the perceived ordeal of switching insurer
Changes in standards or regulations required	Need for approval by Italian regulators of product changes
Internal	
Internal political maneuvering	Existing management may feel threatened
Reluctance or resistance by those needed for active implementation	People comfortable with the established procedures
Resource constraints	Very little budget for intensive lobbying and advertising
Platform changes required	Disconnects between your current capability platforms and any of the following new platforms needed to render your marketbuster deliverable
Human resource and skills platforms	Staffing for call center, Internet Web site, risk analysis, data mining
Logistics platforms	Create call centers, Web site
Distributor platforms	Recruit tied agents
IT and database platforms	Create data-mining database, scalable Web site
Technology platforms	Develop risk analysis tools
Assets, operations, and systems platforms	Royal/agent/employee/customer interfacing capabilities

TABLE 8-2

How Royal Insurance Might Cope with DRAT Challenges

Source	Identify the specific obstacles that will obstruct your marketbuster. Can you use one of the tactics to accelerate implementation?
External	
Powerful incumbents	Threats to tied agents by major insurers. Aggressive countercampaign by incumbents. *Possible tactic:* Mobilize allies in head office?
Opposition from advocacy groups	Pressure on regulators by incumbents. *Possible tactic:* Mobilize allies in EEC?
Risk to key external stakeholders	Overcoming tied-in agents' fear of incumbents, overcoming disinclination to improve service to customers. *Possible tactic:* Lead steer agent? Underwrite agent?
Inertia	Finding way of credibly breaking antipathy. *Possible tactic:* Lead steer customers?
Disruption of customer's system or process	Finding motivation for customer to try Royal. *Possible tactic:* Lead steer customers?
Changes in standards or regulations required	Overcoming very conservative reluctance to approve new products or prices. *Possible tactic:* Mobilize allies in EEC?
Internal	
Internal political maneuvering	Reduce threat for the competent, remove incompetent, bring in outside competents.
Reluctance or resistance by those needed for active implementation	Move comfort line for the competent, move out the incompetent.
Resource constraints	Use guerrilla tactics—start at niche segment with nice, persuadable tied-in agents.
Platform changes required	Disconnects between your current capability platforms and any of the following new platforms needed to render your marketbuster deliverable
Human resource and skills platforms	Recruit and train for staffing needs, using key outsiders with track record.
Logistics platforms	Design scalable system. *Possible tactic:* Mobilize allies in head office with SAS?
Distributor platforms	Start with medium-sized hungry, recruitable tied agents. *Possible tactic:* Pilot with beta agent? Underwrite?
IT and database platforms	Create easily mineable database with user-friendly interface. *Possible tactic:* Pilot with beta agents? Run in parallel?
Technology platforms	Get top-quality data-mining and risk analysis software. *Possible tactic:* Mobilize head office to secure SAS?
Assets, operations, and systems platforms	Design completely new, user-friendly system. *Possible tactic:* Start pilots with beta users and develop operability with their feedback? Underwrite?

TABLE 8-3

Marketbusting Kite for Royal Insurance

Element	Needed to Support the Marketbusting System
Agenda The key things that the critical people spend time on	1. Building customer satisfaction and retention 2. Building the business (new customers, products, services, distribution channels) 3. Building operational excellence through meritocratic pricing 4. Promoting corporate image
Norms What principles and behaviors are valued?	1. Corporate image 2. Transparency of product and services 3. Delivering unequaled customer satisfaction and service 4. Culture of empowerment
News What information and measures are paramount?	1. Customer satisfaction ratings and retention 2. Customer profiles and portfolio 3. Communication with customers 4. Risk profiles and risk selection
Allocations What gets resourced and how are people rewarded?	Resources go to 1. Data management 2. Risk management 3. Call center and Internet Rewards and recognition go for successes at 1. New policies and renewals 2. Passion for finding customer solutions 3. Customer satisfaction scores
Structure Power, authority, responsibility structure	1. Personal responsibility and authority are situated as close to customer as possible 2. Personal responsibility for development of individuals
History Key routines that have developed and drive activities	Customer audit Performance management system for 1. Statistical analysis 2. Decision support 3. Planning and forecasting 4. CRM functionality
Symbols Meaningful actions, ceremonies, icons	1. Carta dei Diritti 2. Carta dei Privilegi 3. Public and personal letter dissemination of PricewaterhouseCoopers audit

We have found that it can take as little as three to four hours to develop the first-cut frame you need for your new kite.

Remember that your kite analysis is meant to focus you on developing a set of core, consistent themes that integrate and align coordinated marketbusting action in your operation. After you have developed these core themes, you can readily identify the obstacles to moving from the current kite to the marketbusting kite. Then you can appoint champions to begin making detailed plans to overcome the obstacles and jointly begin taking coordinated action to effect the marketbusting transition.

Epilogue

In January 2002, Direct Line bought Royal Insurance from Royal & Sun Alliance for slightly less than 20 million euros. As a result of the deal, Direct Line ended up with three hundred thousand subscribers in Italy.

Royal Insurance can rightly take credit for busting a major European insurance market, capitalizing on not just one but several of the marketbusting lenses we have presented in this book.

Taking Your Next Step

Well, there you have it: five lenses, forty moves, and a set of implementation issues to bear in mind as you strive to create exceptional growth in profits and profitability. Now what? Here are a few suggestions:

- Make marketbusting a part of your conversation and your management meetings, and devote at least some of your time to it every week. Set aside some time explicitly for getting away from today's business to think about the future. A simple way to do this? Make a weekly "date" with yourself, and put it in your calendar, with the commitment to think about marketbusting (by which we mean dramatic growth, not the word itself). When you have regular meetings with colleagues, put a marketbusting topic somewhere near the beginning of the agenda. Even if you don't spend much time on it at every meeting, the fact that it is there will keep the topic alive and show that you care about it.

- Test some of the tools we've described here to identify opportunities for marketbusting. Do you see big changes afoot in your regulatory environment, as Mendes did? Consider looking at industry dynamics as a key trigger. Do you think that customers' experiences could be improved? Consumption chain analysis comes to mind. Do you believe that there is an opportunity to radically differentiate your products and services from the competition? Try attribute mapping. Do you think you can win by developing really different ways of operating from those of the competition? Key metrics is a natural. And if you can see your way to capitalize on the confluence of tectonic moves in the marketplace, it could represent a significant opportunity.

- As your business rhythm dictates, begin to plan how you might construct a marketbuster. Use discovery-driven planning to make the concepts crisp.[1] Then work your way through your kite and DRAT tables—not to fall into analysis paralysis, but to make sure you've given the most essential elements some thought in a comprehensive way.

- As you move into execution mode, don't be afraid to redirect the initiative as new information comes in. Try to keep your moves modest and low risk until you have reduced the most significant uncertainties you face. This strategy is a component of "real options" reasoning.[2]

- For easy reference, we've included in the appendix the provocative questions sprinkled throughout this book.

As we bring this book to a close, we thank you for sharing the results of a journey we have been on for the past three years. We appreciate your interest and attention. Even better, we'd love to hear from you. What worked? What didn't? What did you learn? And what would others benefit from hearing about? What more would you like to learn about yourself? These are the issues that keep our research engaging, exciting, and, we hope, useful.

We wish you luck!

The 40 MarketBusting Moves

1. Reconstruct the Consumption Chain

Can links in the existing chain be eliminated or combined with other links?

Can you completely replace this set of links with some other set?

Can you accomplish the same outcome with a different chain?

Can you reshuffle the links to improve your customer's experience?

If parts of the chain are a hassle, can you solve the problem in a different way?

Can you create a complete solution to replace a piecemeal solution?

2. Digitize to Combine or Replace Links in an Existing Chain

Inspect each link in the chain. Can you find ways to deploy Internet, telecommunications, or information technology and thereby dramatically enhance your offering by

Replacing or combining links?

Improving links by making the customer experience better, cheaper, or more convenient?

Capturing and mining data about the market or about your service delivery?

Better managing your logistics?

Adding new links that customers will be willing to pay for?

Creating new offerings from the information you now collect anyway?

3. Make Some Links in the Consumption Chain Smarter

Inspect each major link in your consumption chain. Can you find ways of deploying digital intelligence at that link to make your offering

- More responsive?

- Less of a hassle?

- More informative?

- More fine-tuned?

- More user-friendly?

- More convenient?

and thereby dramatically enhance the quality or convenience of the links in your chain?

Can you use digital intelligence to create greater awareness of the benefits you offer at that link?

Can you use digital intelligence to tell you when a customer is at the trigger point for that link?

4. Eliminate Time Delays in the Links of the Chain

Inspect each major link in your consumption chain.

In some links, are there delays between the time demand occurs and the time delivery is completed?

Are these delays expensive, dangerous, or frustrating for customers?

Are there ways to eliminate or shorten these delays? Are there ways to compensate for them?

Are there ways you can help your customers reduce delays for *their* customers?

5. Monopolize a Trigger Event

Inspect each major trigger in your consumption chain.

How can you position your offering to monopolize a trigger?

Can you be the first to know that a trigger event has occurred?

Can your firm be the first in line or first in the customer's mind when the triggering event occurs?

Can you create triggers that favor your firm or your offering?

6. Dramatically Improve Positives

To determine your offering's positive differentiators, have your customers from the key segment answer the following questions:

Why do they buy from you and not the competition?

What do you offer that they not only like but also are prepared to pay a premium for?

What does your offering do better than anyone else's?

How close is the competition to matching you on these features? Are you progressively reducing the cost of providing these features?

Have your customers from the key segment complete the following sentences:

I would buy (or pay) more if, when I use it, I could . . .

I would buy (or pay) more if, when I buy it, I could . . .

I would buy (or pay) more if, when I select it, I could . . .

7. Eliminate Tolerables or Emerging Dissatisfiers

Tolerables

What are the features that your most important segments would list if you asked them to complete the following sentence: "If only you could eliminate _____ from your offering, I would buy (or pay) a lot more"?

Can you get rid of the tolerables in ways that competitors can't? How?

Are you experiencing increasing complaints about a feature or characteristic?

To what extent are your target customers beginning to compare you to your competition unfavorably with respect to this attribute?

Dissatisfiers

Which attributes do people who interact with customers hear the most grumbling about? Is it something all providers do? Is it something only you do?

Is this attribute increasingly cited as a key reason for customers returning the product or discontinuing the service?

Are any competitors claiming that they are superior with respect to this attribute?

8. Break Up Existing Segments

Underserved Segments

Is there any current or emerging segment that is being underserved by the current attribute maps for major links in the consumption chain?

Are there trends that might give you the opportunity to break apart an existing segment?

Behavioral Segmentation

Have you looked at how various people behave at various links in the chain?

Can you segment by creating a set of attributes that will appeal to the need that customers are seeking to address at the moment that behavior becomes important?

Have you considered common behaviors that cut across demographic segments—for instance, when some customers simply want to be taken care of with little fuss while others prefer a more personal touch?

9. Infuse the Offering with Empathy

Adding Empathy

Can you redesign the offering at any link to make the customer experience more enjoyable?

Can you make the customer feel more satisfied, safer, more confident, less frustrated, more secure, or more amused?

Behavioral Attuning

Are the attributes you offer a good fit for the target segment's behavior?

Have you taken these customers' financial, social, and attitudinal perspectives into account when designing the offering?

10. Add a Compelling Parallel Offering

Direct Customer Benefits

Is there anything you can offer in parallel with your offering that will give you the edge in attracting customers?

Is there anything you can do to make your customers' experience better, even if it doesn't seem to relate to what you produce or do?

Indirect Customer Benefits

Is there any way your company or your offering can be associated with something the customer values?

11. Eliminate Complexity

Are there attributes you could eliminate and thus reduce your cost and potentially the price to the customer?

Are customers complaining about the complexity of your products or services?

Can you readily identify features that many of your target segments don't care about?

12. Capture the Value You Deliver

Customer Takes Offering for Granted

Are you providing an important service or benefit to the customer but are not getting paid for it?

Would the customer *not* buy if you started to charge?

Customer Benefits from Attributes

Can you generate revenues differently—perhaps by menu pricing?

Can you create an *annuity stream*? In other words, is there a way of charging a per-use fee or monthly fee?

13. Radically Change the Unit of Business

Probe the following questions. Keep at it until you are convinced that you have really gotten people to think.

Can you consider how you might generate revenues via a different unit of business?

Can you charge for what you offer in a different way?

Can you incur costs and make payments in a different way?

Can you shift the emphasis in how you charge customers from what you traditionally provide to what they might value (for instance, going from a part of a solution to the actual solution)?

Can you create better incentives for your people by changing the unit of business (for instance, going from an incentive system based on business unit performance to one based on the total relationship between your company and your customer)?

Would some other way of charging for what you sell be more convenient, less effortful, or easier to explain to your customers?

14. Radically Improve Your Productivity

Can you dramatically enhance your productivity by deploying new technology?

- Direct cost productivity
- Fixed cost productivity
- Asset productivity
- Revenue productivity

Can you leapfrog your competition in productivity? Look especially for situations where their resources are already committed to something else (such as integrating a large merger).

Can you eliminate time-wasting repetitive activities to enhance productivity?

Can you figure out how to eliminate transactions costs (such as internal reviews and approvals) by automating some of your internal control practices thus boosting productivity?

15. Improve Your Cash Flow Velocity

How might you accelerate the cash flow velocity of your firm?

Could you eliminate or reduce inventory?

Might you delay payments to others?

Can you speed up receipts from your customers?

Can you generate cash before you have to incur costs (such as with Dell's "build to order" computers)?

Can you speed up the ordering cycle of your customers?

Can you get paid more frequently over the lifetime of a contract?

Can you automate the payment stream so that manual delays don't hold up incoming cash?

Can you make sure that your invoicing mechanisms are easy for your customers to respond to, so that you don't create additional payment delays?

Have you checked to see whether you might link up with customers electronically to speed payments?

Have you explored technologies such as direct-deposit or lockboxes to speed payments?

16. Change the Way You Use Assets

Can you reduce the asset intensity of your business by outsourcing some activities to specialist providers?

Can you eliminate the need to own certain assets?

Can you utilize assets owned by someone else on an as-needed basis?

Can you use assets more effectively—for instance, by extending the time of day in which they are used or by using remote electronics to operate them?

Might you be able to pool your assets with those of other firms and reduce the asset intensity for the whole group?

Can you change fixed assets to variable assets, for instance by establishing utilization contracts with suppliers for certain services?

Can you help your customers reduce their fixed asset burden by taking on their assets and charging them for usage?

17. Improve Your Customers' Key Metrics

Have your marketbusting team gather the following information:

What are the key numbers your customers seek to achieve? (Be explicit.)

How do your customers measure this outcome?

What are the key ratios in your customers' businesses?

What are some ways to

- Help your customers improve their key ratios (financial, operating, investment)?

- Conceive of a better way to help customers hit the numbers they care about (market share, cash flow, EBITDA, revenue growth, profit)?

- Help customers better understand what really drives success in their businesses?

Can you find ways to improve your customers' productivity?

Can you help customers make better use of their assets? Their working capital?

Can you take over some aspect of your customers' operations that they find burdensome?

18. Improve Your Customers' Personal Productivity

Can you change the way you do business to save your customers time?

Can you reduce the number of steps a customer must take to do business with you?

Can you eliminate hassles and annoyances in your transactions (for instance, forcing the customer to repeat information on forms, to collect information from different places, or to get material from third parties before they can do business with you)?

Can you create a single point of interface between your company and your customers?

Can you address some customer issues with a single interaction rather than with multiple interactions?

Can you routinize customer-facing activities to make them faster?

Can you find ways to improve the personal productivity of your customers' staff? On the job? In their private lives?

19. Help Improve Your Customers' Cash Flow

Refer to the questions in #15 with respect to your cash flow velocity. Ask also:

Can you change the way you do business to help customers get revenues in more quickly or delay expenditures?

Can you help customers better coordinate their activities to eliminate cash flow losses due to internal inefficiencies?

Can you change the way you do business to make some fixed costs variable for your customer?

Can you eliminate "nuisance" payments for your customers?

20. Help Improve Your Customers' Quality

Can you redesign the way you do business with customers to help them improve quality metrics?

Can you offer examples or advice to customers to help them improve quality?

Can you offer consulting solutions to improve customer quality (or related concepts such as safety)?

Can you lead your industry in creating more high-quality offerings than it does today?

Can you provide quality-oriented feedback to your customers so that they can respond in real time?

21. End-Run Predictable Industry Swings

22. Capitalize on Second-Order Effects of Industry Cycles

23. Launch a Disruptive Response to Cycles

For moves 21, 22, and 23, examine your industry's sales over at least the past decade, looking for cyclical patterns. With this information in mind, brainstorm answers to the following questions:

What bottlenecks are likely to occur in the cyclical peaks?

What surpluses are likely to occur in the troughs?

Are there ways to end-run swings in the industry by positioning your firm to exploit bottlenecks during peak demand and to avoid troughs?

What second-order effects will cyclical swings have on the industry?

What second-order demands or surpluses will be created? For you? For members of the industry value chain, such as suppliers and distributors?

Are there opportunities to introduce innovations that mute or eliminate the impact of cycles?

24. Exploit Shifts in Industry Constraints or Barriers

25. Capitalize on Second-Order Effects of Shifts in Constraints

26. Use a Shift in a Key Constraint to Disrupt the Industry

For moves 24, 25, and 26, list the most important constraints or barriers that have bounded the competition in your industry. Identify those that are or likely will be under pressure to change. Brainstorm those constraints and barriers for answers to the following questions:

Is there a way of capitalizing on this shift by exploiting the new competitive opportunities that it creates?

What are the second-order effects that this shift will create in your industry? In the value chain that supports it?

Can you exploit these second-order effects by making a market-busting move?

Can you exploit this shift to disrupt the way competitors compete?

27. Exploit Your Industry's Structure for the Next Life Cycle Stage

28. Understand the Second-Order Effects of the Next Stage

29. Redirect, Disrupt, or Alter the Evolutionary Trajectory

For moves 27, 28, and 29, examine the evolution of your product life cycle, and identify the ways competitors have converged in the current stage of the industry's evolution. Look for indicators that this convergence is vulnerable to a competitive format that will move the industry into the next life cycle stage. Have your team begin to probe whether there are opportunities to capitalize on life cycle shifts:

Are there places (proliferation of product models, emergence of dominant design, preemptive roll-up, or consolidation) where you can anticipate and capture first-mover advantages by pre-emptive evolutionary moves?

Can you anticipate second-order effects of industry evolution by pinpointing places where industry fragmentation, disintermediation, or concentration creates marketbusting opportunities?

Are there ways you might be able to move boldly to redirect, alter, or disrupt the current course of the industry?

30. Exploit a Shift in the Value Chain

31. Exploit Second-Order Effects of Shifts in the Value Chain

32. Reduce Costs or Abolish Bottlenecks to Disrupt the Value Chain

For moves 30, 31, and 32, examine the value chain of your industry, reviewing how it has changed and how its value-capture patterns are shifting. Use your insights to seek marketbusting opportunities to capture value or relocate your participation at emergent shifts in the chain:

Can you spot places to exploit shifts that are occurring or will occur in the value chain structure?

Can you pinpoint second-order consequences up and down the chain where you can reposition your participation?

Can you spot places where you can disrupt the current value chain and change it in ways that suit you?

33. Shift the Dimension of Merit

Have you uncovered a new dimension of competing that is different from the current standard modes of competing?

Will it appeal to a large or growing segment of the market that is unimpressed with the current competitive criteria?

Are competitors largely wedded to the current criteria?

Has the very success of an existing solution created new problems that you might address?

34. Create a Market via Cautious Evangelism

Have you uncovered a potential offering that will significantly attend to a problem that is not serviced for a large emergent segment of the market?

Can you present your revised solution in a way that lets you thoroughly test market reaction before you commit major resources?

Are you convinced that this offering will be insulated from rapid matching by entrenched or emergent players?

35. Build a Better Mousetrap

Have you identified an offering that is demonstrably superior on a dimension that is demonstrably attractive to an emergent segment of the market?

If the offering is not demonstrably attractive, can you deliver it at a lower price and still make good money?

36. Undertake Inventive Missionary Work

Can you identify places in which large target segments are persistently unhappy with existing solutions? Have you got a potential solution that might work?

Will you be able to build a technically successful offering at limited cost and incrementally introduce it to clearly identified beta-friendly customers?

Can the process of market education and product development be unfolded without major initial resource commitments?

37. Make a Land Grab

As you evaluate the trends in your markets, are new needs emerging that you might have a solution to address?

Are there growing areas of persistent unhappiness or unease among your target segments?

Have segments become newly aware of social or other issues that might prompt a change in their behavior (such as certain industry categories falling out of favor, new health concerns, social changes with respect to acceptable behavior, and so on)?

Are you sure that your solution works for the target segment? Has it been validated by the market?

Do you know how to advertise, promote, distribute, and service the market? Do you need to do it yourself, or can you use existing infrastructure?

38. Create a Niche to Win

Can you identify small markets with new needs that are wealthy enough to afford to have the need met?

Have you developed something new in terms of products or services that might prove compelling to a customer group you have not served before?

Is the initial market large enough to minimize cash burn, or will you be able to capitalize on a large long-term market? If so, can you gain rapid dominance of the emerging market and lock out competitors?

Can you protect the long-term market well enough that you can build it without losing your profits to competitors?

39. Run the Arms Race

Are you confident that you can get a reliable solution in place quickly and profitably?

Are you being encouraged by the target segment to attend to this problem?

Are these customers willing to place advance orders at good prices? Do you have a win-win?

Are they willing to take on beta models and learn with you?

Will you be able to protect your long-term position?

40. Bet on Blue Sky Ventures

Has no other approach recommended in this book shown you a less risky alternative, or are you so convinced of the enormous upside that you simply must go for this particular brass ring?

What evidence do you have of a huge upside, a controllable downside, and the sustainability of future profits?

NOTES

Chapter 1

1. McGrath, R. G., and I. C. MacMillan (2000). *The Entrepreneurial Mindset: Strategies for Continuously Creating Opportunity in an Age of Uncertainty.* Boston: Harvard Business School Press.

2. Christensen, C. (1997). *The Innovator's Dilemma: When New Technologies Cause Great Firms to Fail.* Boston: Harvard Business School Press. Christensen, C. M., and M. E. Raynor (2003). *The Innovator's Solution: Creating and Sustaining Successful Growth.* Boston: Harvard Business School Press.

3. MacMillan, I. C., and R. G. McGrath (1996). Discover your products' hidden potential. *Harvard Business Review* 74 (May–June). MacMillan, I. C., and R. McGrath (1997). Discovering new points of differentiation. Harvard Business Review 75 (July–August): 133–145.

4. McGrath, R. G. (1999). Falling forward: Real options reasoning and entrepreneurial failure. *Academy of Management Review* 24(1): 13–30.

5. Pietersen, W. (2002). *Reinventing Strategy: Using Strategic Learning to Create and Sustain Breakthrough Performance.* New York: Wiley.

6. MacMillan, I. C., A. Van Putten, et al. (2003). Global gamesmanship. *Harvard Business Review* 81(5): 62–71.

7. Baumol, W. J. (2002). *The Free-Market Innovation Machine: Analyzing the Growth Miracle of Capitalism.* Princeton, NJ: Princeton University Press.

8. Block, Z., and I. C. MacMillan (1993). *Corporate Venturing: Creating New Businesses Within the Firm.* Boston: Harvard Business School Press. Leifer, R., C. McDermott, et al. (2000). *Radical Innovation: How Mature Companies Can Outsmart Upstarts.* Boston: Harvard Business School Press.

9. Sitkin, S. B. (1992). Learning through failure: The strategy of small losses. *Research in Organizational Behavior* 14: 231–266. Farson, R., and R. Keyes (2002). The failure tolerant leader. *Harvard Business Review* 80(8): 64–71. Matta, N. F.,

and R. N. Ashkenas (2003). Why good projects fail anyway. *Harvard Business Review* 81(9): 109–114.

10. Peters, T., and R. Waterman (1982). *In Search of Excellence: Lessons from America's Best-Run Companies.* New York: Harper & Row.

11. Miller, D. (1990). *The Icarus Paradox: How Exceptional Companies Bring About Their Own Downfall: New Lessons in the Dynamics of Corporate Success, Decline, and Renewal.* New York: HarperBusiness.

Chapter 2

1. MacMillan, I. C., and R. G. McGrath (1996). Discover your products' hidden potential. *Harvard Business Review* 74.

2. Credit Suisse First Boston (2000). Logistics in the Digital Economy: A Comprehensive Overview of Outsourced Logistics.

3. Anderson, J. C., and J. A. Narus (1998). Business marketing: Understand what customers value. *Harvard Business Review* 76: 5–15. Wise, R., and P. Baumgartner (1999). Go downstream: The new profit imperative in manufacturing. *Harvard Business Review* 77(5): 133. Zook, C., and J. Allen (2003). Growth outside the core. *Harvard Business Review* 81(12): 66.

4. Waters, C. D. (2001). Wireless handhelds help speed table service. *Nation's Restaurant News* 35(12): 26. Frumkin, P. (2002). Operators say handheld systems provide benefits for wait staff, customers. *Nation's Restaurant News* 36(46): 36.

5. Weinstein, D. (1997). Start-up success story. *U.S. 1 Newspaper,* November 19.

Chapter 3

1. MacMillan, I. C., and R. McGrath (1997). Discovering new points of differentiation. *Harvard Business Review* 75: 133–145.

2. Lowry, T. (2002). The sinkhole of synergy: A review of *Bamboozled at the Revolution: How Big Media Lost Billions in the Battle for the Internet,* by John Motavalli. *Business Week* 22.

3. Berner, R. (2002). Why P&G's smile is so bright. *Business Week,* 12 August: 58–60.

4. Jackson, B. (2001). In the sport of kings, a bootstrap success. *U.S. 1 Newspaper,* March 21.

5. Hafner, Katie (2002). Tech gizmos torturing users < http://www.silicon valley.com/mld/siliconvalley/3188793.htm > (accessed 12 July 2002).

Chapter 4

1. Dixit, A. K., and R. S. Pindyck (1994). *Investment Under Uncertainty.* Princeton, New Jersey: Princeton University Press.

2. Johnson, J. T. (2004). Distribution online: Dawn of a new era. *Network World* 21(36): 34.

3. Mullaney, T.J., H. Green, M. Arndt, R. D. Hof, and L. Himelstein (2003). The e-biz surprise. It wasn't all hype. *Business Week,* 12 May: 60.

4. McGrath, R. G., and I. C. MacMillan (2000). *The Entrepreneurial Mindset: Strategies for Continuously Creating Opportunity in an Age of Uncertainty.* Boston: Harvard Business School Press.

5. Mullaney et al. The e-biz surprise.

6. Hutton, A. (2001). Four rules for taking your message to Wall Street. *Harvard Business Review* (May): 5–11.

7. Kaplan, S. (2001). Concrete ideas. *CIO Magazine,* 15 August.

8. In uncertain markets it is sometimes difficult to determine which firms constitute your industry. In this case, try to identify the companies you consider your most serious competitors.

9. If you have no hard data but can make reasonable estimates, use these. Otherwise, too bad—life is never simple.

10. *Business Wire.* (2002). Fitch upgrades Cemex to "BBB" from "BBB-": Outlook Stable.

11. Microsoft Corporation (2001). Lamons Gasket Company—Industrial supplier deploys B2B E-commerce solution in 90 days using Microsoft supplier enablement solution < http://www.microsoft.com/resources/casestudies/casestudy. asp?casestudyid = 11766&PF = yes > (accessed September 26, 2004).

12. Ibid.

13. < http://www.federalreserve.gov/releases/h15/data/m/tcm10y.txt > (accessed September 2004).

14. EBITDA stands for earnings before interest and taxes plus depreciation and amortization.

15. < http://arstechnica.com/news/posts/20040630-3951.html > (accessed September 2004).

Chapter 5

1. Ghemawat, P. (1984). Capacity expansion in the titanium dioxide industry. *Journal of Industrial Economics* 33: 145–163.

2. Kogut, B., and N. Kulatilaka (1994). Operating flexibility, global manufacturing, and the option value of a multinational network. *Management Science* 40(1): 123–139.

3. Sanchez, R., and J. T. Mahoney (1996). Modularity, flexibility, and knowledge management in product and organizational design. *Strategic Management Journal* 17: 63–76. Baldwin, C., and K. B. Clark (2000). *Design Rules: The Power of Modularity.* Cambridge, MA: MIT Press.

4. Suarez, F. F., and J. M. Utterback (1995). Dominant designs and the survival of firms. *Strategic Management Journal* 16: 415–430.

5. Utterback, J. M., and W. J. Abernathy (1975). A dynamic model of process and product innovation. *Omega* 3(6): 639–656. Aldrich, H. E., and C. M. Fiol (1994). Fools rush in? The institutional context of industry creation. *Academy of Management Review* 19(4): 645–670. Aldrich, H. (1999). *Organizations Evolving.* Thousand Oaks, CA: Sage Publications. Moore, G. A. (2000). *Living on the Fault Line: Managing for Shareholder Value in the Age of the Internet.* New York: Harper Business.

6. Tushman, M., and P. Anderson (1986). Technological discontinuities and organizational environments. *Administrative Science Quarterly* 31: 439–465. Harrigan, K. R. (1990). Will you be "the last iceman"? *Sales & Marketing Management* (January): 62–67. Cooper, A. C., and C. G. Smith (1992). How established firms respond to threatening technologies. *Academy of Management Executive* 6(2): 55–70.

7. Porter, M. (1980). *Competitive Strategy: Techniques for Analyzing Industries and Competitors.* New York: The Free Press.

8. Sahlman, W. A., and H. Stevenson (1985). Capital market myopia. *Journal of Business Venturing* 1: 7–30.

9. Kulatilaka, N., and L. Trigeorgis (1994). The general flexibility to switch: Real options revisited. *International Journal of Finance* 6(2): 778–798.

10. Lorenzoni, G., and O. Ornati (1988). Constellations of firms and new ventures. *Journal of Business Venturing* 3: 41–57.

11. Port, O., I. M. Kunii, B. Einhorn, and A. Park (2002). Chips on monster wafers: How the shift to larger wafers and thin circuits will transform the industry. *Business Week,* 11 November: 50–53.

12. Maloney, D. (2001). Pioneer-standard blazes a new trail. *Modern Materials Handling* 56(4): 73–77.

13. *BusinessWeek Online* (2003). Hot growth 2003 scoreboard < http://bwnt. businessweek.com/hot_growth/2003/index.asp >.

14. Goodman, M. (2000). U.S. and the Americas Investment Perspectives. Morgan Stanley Analyst Report, 2 August, and personal correspondence, M. Goodman, 1 October 2004.

15. Harrigan, K. R. (1980). *Strategies for Declining Businesses.* Lexington, MA: Lexington Books.

16. Quinn, R. E., and K. Cameron (1983). Organizational life cycles and shifting criteria of effectiveness: Some preliminary evidence. *Management Science* 29(1): 33–50.

17. Proctor, T. (2001). Corporate restructuring: The pitfalls of changing industry structure. *Management Decision* 39(3): 197–204.

18. Moore, *Living on the Fault Line.*

19. Dorsch, Jeff. (1999) Hitachi joins the crowd. *Electronic News,* 7 June. DPI readies Singapore mask shop (1999). *Electronic News,* 1 November. Du Pont Photomask press release (1996). < www.photomask.com >, 5 January.

20. Christensen, C. (1997). *The Innovator's Dilemma: When New Technologies Cause Great Firms to Fail*. Boston, MA; Harvard Business School Press.

21. Mosquera, M. (2001). Bayer taps SAP to speed distribution: Drug maker leans on ERP system to meet spikes in demand following the anthrax scare. *InternetWeek*, 10 December: 31–32.

22. MBNA Corporation (2002). Hoovers Online < http://premium.hoovers.com/subscribe/co/factsheet.xhtml?COID = 12449 >.

23. Fisher, D. (1998). Sweet consolation. *Forbes* 162(6). Kinder Morgan Energy Partners (2002). About us. < www.kindermorgan.com/about_us/ >. Taylor, G. (2002). Kinder Morgan Plans $43 Million Expansion. *Chemical Market Reporter*, 11 January. Womack, Anita (1998). Where can affinity programs take you? *Bank Marketing*.

Chapter 6

1. Tushman, M., and P. Anderson (1986). Technological discontinuities and organizational environments. *Administrative Science Quarterly* 31: 439–465. Henderson, R. M., and K. B. Clark (1990). Architectural innovation: The reconfiguration of existing product technologies and the failure of established firms. *Administrative Science Quarterly* 35: 9–30.

2. Block, Z., and I. C. MacMillan (1993). *Corporate Venturing: Creating New Businesses Within the Firm*. Boston: Harvard Business School Press. Christensen, C. M., and M. E. Raynor (2003). *The Innovator's Solution: Creating and Sustaining Successful Growth*. Boston: Harvard Business School Press.

3. Cyert, R. M., and J. G. March (1963). *A Behavioral Theory of the Firm*. Englewood Cliffs, NJ,: Prentice-Hall.

4. Van de Ven, A., H. Angle, and M. S. Poole (1989). *Research on the Management of Innovation: The Minnesota Studies*. New York: Harper & Row Ballinger Division. Schoemaker, P., and C. A. J. M. v. d. Heijden (1992). Integrating scenarios into strategic planning at Royal Dutch/Shell. *Planning Review*, May/June: 41–46. Heijden, K. A. v. d., and NetLibrary Inc. (2002). *The Sixth Sense: Accelerating Organisational Learning with Scenarios*. Chichester, U.K.: Wiley. Lynn, G., J. G. Morone, and A. S. Paulson (1996). Marketing and discontinuous innovation: the probe and learn process. *California Management Review* 38(3): 8–37. Leifer, R., C. McDermott, et al. (2000). *Radical Innovation: How Mature Companies Can Outsmart Upstarts*. Boston: Harvard Business School Press.

5. Schoonhoven, C. B., and R. Romanelli (2001). *The Entrepreneurship Dynamic: Origins of Entrepreneurship and the Evolution of Industries*. Stanford, CA: Stanford University Press. Keil, T. (2002). *External Corporate Venturing: Strategic Renewal in Rapidly Changing Industries*. Westport, CT: Quorum Books.

6. Jim Carnes, on being, and remaining, a high-tech state (2001). *Business News New Jersey*, 23 October: 13.

7. Dougherty, D. (1990). Understanding new markets for new products. *Strategic Management Journal* 11: 59–78.

8. Dos Santos, B. L., and K. Peffers (1995). Rewards to investors in innovative information technology applications: First movers and early followers in ATMs. *Organization Science* 6(3): 241–259.

9. Christensen, C. (1997). *The Innovator's Dilemma: When New Technologies Cause Great Firms to Fail*. Boston, MA: Harvard Business School Press Christensen and Raynor, *The Innovator's Solution*.

10. This discussion assumes relatively free markets, with firms motivated to innovate in order to gain from proprietary access to the solution that emerges.

11. Walras, L. 1984. *Elements of Pure Economics or the Theory of Social Wealth* (W. Jaffe, Trans.). Philadelphia, PA: Orion Editions.

12. Longman, P. (2004). *The Empty Cradle: How Falling Birthrates Threaten World Prosperity and What to Do about It*. New York: Basic Books.

13. For this kind of analysis see Schoemaker, P. S., and R. Gunther (2002). *Profiting from Uncertainty: Strategies for Succeeding No Matter What the Future Brings*. New York: The Free Press.

14. Anderson, P., and M. L. Tushman (1990). Technological discontinuities and dominant designs: A cyclical model of technological change. *Administrative Science Quarterly* 35: 604–633.

15. Centers for Disease Control (2002). BMI: Body Mass Index < http://www.cdc.gov/nccdphp/dnpa/bmi/ >

16. Hoovers Online (2002). Doctors Associates < http://premium.hoovers.com/subscribe/co/factsheet.xhtml?COID = 40450 > (accessed July 12, 2002).

17. Huget, Jennifer L. (2002). Healthy fast foods—for adults. *The Washington Post,* 14 May, HE01.

18. Bowman, E. H., and D. Hurry (1993). Strategy through the option lens: An integrated view of resource investments and the incremental-choice process. *Academy of Management Review* 18(4): 760–782. MacMillan, I. C., and R. G. McGrath (2002). Crafting R&D project portfolios. *Research-Technology Management* 45(5): 48–59.

19. Fifties Web Index (2002). Swanson TV dinners < www.fiftiesweb.com/pop/tv-dinner.htm >.

20. Kleinman, Mark (2001). Nicorette in "quit smoking" DM. *Marketing*.

21. Nicorette (2002). < www.nicorette.com >.

22. Ibid.

23. Rock, Andrea (1999). Quitting time for smokers. *Money* 28(1).

24. "Nicorette poised to rework brand identity globally" (2001). *Marketing*.

25. Woo, C. Y., and A. C. Cooper (1981). Strategies of effective low share businesses. *Strategic Management Journal* 2: 301–318.

26. Block, Z., and I. C. MacMillan (1993). *Corporate Venturing: Creating New Businesses Within the Firm*. Boston: Harvard Business School Press. Leifer et al.,

Radical Innovation. McGrath, R. G., and I. C. MacMillan (2000). *The Entrepreneurial Mindset: Strategies for Continuously Creating Opportunity in an Age of Uncertainty.* Boston: Harvard Business School Press.

Chapter 7

1. Bossidy, L., and R. Charan (2002). *Execution: The Discipline of Getting Things Done.* New York: Crown Business.
2. Galbraith, J. (1973). *Designing Complex Organizations.* Reading, MA,: Addison-Wesley. Nohria, N., W. Joyce, and B. Roberson (2003). What really works. *Harvard Business Review* 81(7): 42–52.
3. Dutton, J. E., S. J. Ashford, K. A. Lawrence, and K. Miner-Rubino (2002). Red light, green light: Making sense of the organizational context for issue selling. *Organization Science* 13(4): 355. Dutton, J. E., and S. E. Jackson (1987). Categorizing strategic issues: Links to organizational action. *Academy of Management Review* 12(1): 76.
4. Miller, G. A. (1956). The magical number seven, plus or minus two: Some limits on our capacity for processing information. *Psychological Review* 63: 81–97.
5. Collins, J. (2001). Level 5 leadership: The triumph of humility and fierce resolve. *Harvard Business Review*, January, 67–76.
6. O'Reilly, C. (1989). Corporations, culture, and commitment: Motivation and social control in organizations. *California Management Review*, summer, 9–25. Saxenian, A. (1994). *Regional Advantage: Culture and Competition in Silicon Valley and Route 128.* Cambridge, MA.: Harvard University Press. Goffee, R., and G. Jones (1998). *The Character of a Corporation: How Your Company's Culture Can Make or Break Your Business.* New York: HarperBusiness.
7. Sitkin, S. B. (1992). Learning through failure: The strategy of small losses. *Research in Organizational Behavior* 14: 231–266. McGrath, R. G. (1999). Falling forward: Real options reasoning and entrepreneurial failure. *Academy of Management Review* 24(1): 13–30. Farson, R., and R. Keyes (2002). The failure tolerant leader. *Harvard Business Review* 80(8): 64–71. Matta, N. F., and R. N. Ashkenas (2003). Why good projects fail anyway. *Harvard Business Review* 81(9): 109–114.
8. Kahneman, D., P. Slovic, and A. Tversky (1982). *Judgment under Uncertainty: Heuristics and Biases.* Cambridge, U.K.; New York: Cambridge University Press.
9. Coser, L. (1959). *The Functions of Social Conflict.* Glencoe, IL,: Free Press. Janis, I. L. (1972). *Victims of Groupthink; a Psychological Study of Foreign-Policy Decisions and Fiascoes.* Boston: Houghton Mifflin. Harvey, J. B. (1974). The Abilene paradox: The management of agreement. *Organizational Dynamics,* Summer. McGrath, R. G., and I. C. MacMillan (1995). Discovery-driven planning. *Harvard Business Review* 73(4): 44–54. Amason, A. C. (1996). Distinguishing the effects of functional and dysfunctional conflict on strategic decision-making: Resolving a paradox for top management teams. *Academy of Management Journal* 39: 123–148.

10. Charan, R. (2001). Conquering a culture of indecision. *Harvard Business Review* 79(4): 74.

11. Kaplan, R. S., and D. P. Norton (1992). The balanced scorecard: Measures that drive performance. *Harvard Business Review* 70: 71–79.

12. Conger, J. A. (1998). The necessary art of persuasion. *Harvard Business Review* 76(3): 84.

13. Pottruck, D. S., and T. Pearce (2000). *Clicks and Mortar: Passion Driven Growth in an Internet Driven World.* San Francisco: Jossey Bass.

14. Beer, M., and N. Nohria (2000). *Breaking the Code of Change.* Boston: Harvard Business School Press.

15. Kerr, J., and J. W. Slocum (1987). Managing corporate culture through reward systems. *Academy of Management Executive* 1(2): 99–108. Kerr, S. (1997). *Ultimate Rewards: What Really Motivates People to Achieve.* Boston: Harvard Business School Press.

16. Bower, J. L. (1970). Managing the resource allocation process: A study of corporate planning and investment. Boston: Division of Research, Graduate School of Business Administration, Harvard University.

17. Pietersen, W. (2002). *Reinventing Strategy: Using Strategic Learning to Create and Sustain Breakthrough Performance.* New York: Wiley.

18. Hope, J., and R. Fraser (2003). *Beyond Budgeting: How Managers Can Break Free from the Annual Performance Trap.* Boston: Harvard Business School Press. Hope, J., and R. Fraser (2003). Who needs budgets? Harvard Business Review 81(2): 108-115.

19. Ibid.

20. Feldman, M. S., and J. G. March (1981). Information in organizations as signal and symbol. *Administrative Science Quarterly* 26: 171–186.

21. McGrath and MacMillan, Discovery-driven planning.

Chapter 8

1. McGrath, R. G., and I. C. MacMillan (1995). Discovery-driven planning. *Harvard Business Review* 73(4): 44–54.

2. MacMillan, I. C., and R. G. McGrath (2002). Crafting R&D project portfolios. *Research-Technology Management* 45(5): 48–59.

INDEX

ACKNOWLEDGMENTS

We were fortunate during the course of this research to be able to take shameless advantage of the talents of our group of student research assistants. They aided the project in innumerable ways, from gathering case data and examples to performing data analyses to conducting interviews. We would like to specifically acknowledge their help and thank them. The students who worked on the project include Jeffery Bonaldi, Karl Boog, Justin Chang, Joon Choi, Francesca Codrea, Elizabeth Esrov, Nihaar Gupta, Justin Heyman, Lindsay Hunt, Alexander Kristofcak, Iris Lin, Kelly Merritt, Beth Mlynarczyk, Tarek Mohamed, Tambu Munhutu, Nicholas Sabin, Sarah Sugarman, Zuzana Vojtekova, and Leslie Yen. James Thompson was instrumental in making sure that we had a good mix of projects and examples.

We both depend on Roz Cohen to a significant extent. Aside from her administrative role at the Sol C. Snider Entrepreneurial Center, she hires our researchers, keeps projects moving, and in general takes responsibility for day-to-day operations. We are very grateful for her consistent, proactive, and empathic efforts on our behalf.

Many of the best ideas in the book derive from the experiences and insights of practitioners who have supported our research and who have implemented the concepts in practice. Many wonderful leaders in companies have been important to our work. In particular, we would like to recognize Margaret Alldredge, Birgit Byman-Kivivuori, Tom Connolly, Bob Cooper, Manfred Eiden, Barry Frylinck, Bob Goergen, Tony Isaacs, Cindy Johnson, Dan McGrath, Stephen Newman, Takeru Ohe, Prisca Peyer-Ehrbar, Ron Pierantozzi, Bob Prince, John Rainieri, Claudio R. Rodriguez, Tom Roy, Petri Salonen, and Helena Terho.

Finally, Rita in particular would like to express appreciation for the support and camaraderie of her colleagues at Columbia Executive Education. Thanks to all of you for making it fun to come to work.

ABOUT THE AUTHORS

Rita Gunther McGrath joined the faculty of Columbia Business School, where she is currently an Associate Professor, in 1993. Prior to life in academia, she was an IT director, worked in the political arena, and founded two start-ups.

McGrath is best known for helping companies discover and capitalize on growth opportunities. Her research addresses technological innovation, entrepreneurship, and corporate venturing. She publishes widely in leading academic journals such as the *Strategic Management Journal, Academy of Management Review, Academy of Management Journal,* and *Management Science.* The Strategic Management Society presented her with the McKinsey best paper award in 2001 and an honorable mention for best paper in 2004. She also received the Maurice Holland award from the Industrial Research Institute for the best paper published in *Research Technology Management* (2000). Previous awards include the *Academy of Management Review* best paper award (1999), the Entrepreneurship Theory and Practice Award for the Best Conceptual Paper (both 1992 and 1996), and the European Foundation for Entrepreneurship Research (EFER) award for the best paper of 1995. She is on the editorial boards of the *Academy of Management Review,* the *Strategic Management Journal,* and the *Journal of Business Venturing.* She is a Director of the Strategic Management Society, the premier professional organization for strategists.

In her research and consulting, she has worked with companies such as 3M, Nokia, DuPont, the Kone Corporation of Finland, Deutsche Telekom, the Japan Bank for International Cooperation, Swiss Reinsurance, Inc., and many others. She is also active in Columbia Business School Executive Education (http://www.gsb. columbia.edu/execed). She is the Faculty Director for the programs Creating Breakthrough Strategy, Executing Breakthrough Strategy, and Leading Strategic Growth and Change.

Ian MacMillan is the Academic Director of the Sol C. Snider Entrepreneurial Research Programs at the Wharton School, University of Pennsylvania. He is also the Fred Sullivan Professor in the Management Department. Formerly he was Director of the Entrepreneurship Center at New York University and a teacher at Columbia and Northwestern Universities and the University of South Africa. In 1999 he was awarded the Swedish Foundation for Small Business Research Prize for his contribution to research in entrepreneurship.

Prior to joining the academic world, MacMillan was a chemical engineer and gained experience in gold and uranium mining, chemical and explosives manufacturing, oil refining, and soap and food production, and was a scientist at the South African Atomic Energy Board. He has been a director of several companies in the travel, import/export, and pharmaceutical industries. He also has extensive consulting experience, having worked with companies such as Air Products, DuPont, General Electric, GTE, IBM, Citibank, Chubb & Son, American Re-Insurance, Texas Instruments, KPMG, Hewlett-Packard, Intel, Fluor Daniel, Matsushita (Japan), Olympus (Japan), and L. G. Group (Korea), among others.

MacMillan's articles have appeared in the *Harvard Business Review, Sloan Management Review, Journal of Business Venturing, Administrative Science Quarterly, Academy of Management Journal, Academy of Management Review, Academy of Management Executive, Management Science,* and *Strategic Management Journal,* among others.